I *knit* NEW YORK

VOLUME ONE

ONE MORE ROW PRESS

New York • Washington

One More Row Press

Editors: Kathleen Dames & Alice O'Reilly
Pattern & Product Photographer: Gale Zucker
Art Director & Graphic Designer: Kathleen Dames
Technical Editors: Corrina Ferguson, Liz Rolle
Illustrator: Laurel Johnson

Photographer's Assistant: Yliana Tibitoski
Model: Rebecca Fox
New York City Photographers: Kathleen Dames, Alice O'Reilly

Yarn Support: Alice O'Reilly/Backyard Fiberworks

Printed in the United States

Direct all inquiries to *hello@onemorerowpress.com*

Website: *onemorerowpress.com*
Instagram: *@onemorerowpress*
Pinterest: *onemorerowpress*

Contents

Hello, Knit Yorker!*

Alternative NYC greetings include "Yo!", "I'm walkin' here!", and "Hey, watch it!"

What says "New York" to you? We asked a few of our favorite New Yorkers to answer that question in knits and purls. Whether you think of the Big Apple in terms of history or landmarks, the movies or celestial events, we've got something for you.

But we wanted to bring you more than just a gorgeous pattern collection. What is it like to be a knitter in New York (a Knit Yorker, if you will)? **Kay Gardiner**, the Northern half of *Mason-Dixon Knitting*, spins a tale of knitting in the "dark ages," while *Indie Untangled* founder **Lisa Chamoff** takes you on a multiborough yarn crawl. Then go on a #buttonhunt through the Garment District and beyond with **Kathleen Dames**, cocreator of *I Knit New York*, knitwear designer, and host of *The Sweater with Kathleen Dames*.

Every pattern in this collection shows off the gorgeous colors and bases **Alice O'Reilly**, cocreator of *I Knit New York*, curated for her beloved yarn line **Backyard Fiberworks**. Learn more about her approach to color theory and each of the delicious yarns used in this collection.

We are thrilled to share **Brittney Bailey**'s lace beanie and funnel-neck pullover; **Kathleen Dames**'s lace cardigan, cowl and gloves set, and cabled stole; **Kirsten Kapur**'s three-color shawl; **Xandy Peters**'s reversible top; and **Lars Rains**'s cabled hat, colorwork hat, and short-row cowl. Which one is your favorite?

Happy knitting!

Alice + Kathleen

Editors, One More Row Press

P.S. Where shall **One More Row Press** go in the future? Drop us a note at *hello@onemorerowpress.com*. Or which New York icons do you want to knit next? Tell us! We're already talking about knitting *More* New York.

Knitting in "Old" New York

Kay Gardiner

New York City is many things, but it doesn't generally spring to mind as a place where knitting and other cozy crafts take root and flourish. But New York City, in the 1990s, was where I got bitten, bad, by the knitting bug.

On an early spring Saturday, I was walking up Broadway after a run in Central Park, stretching my legs and looking for carbs. In the low 80s, a sign by a door buzzer caught my eye: The Yarn Company, it said. Up one flight.

For no reason other than maybe idle curiosity, I climbed the steep, lumpily carpeted stairs of a walkup building, and entered a cave of color. The walls of the shop were lined with shelves bursting with skeins and hanks and balls of yarn in every shade, from NYC black-with-a-pop-of-charcoal to vivid reds, blues, and greens. There were tweeds, and there were crazy multicolored yarns, the likes of which I'd never seen before.

over by lorgnetted ladies who were often crabby even by New York standards.

My favorite shop, gone for years now, was a Dickensian enterprise on the second floor, above a derelict hairdresser's shop on Madison Avenue in the 30s, across the street from the Morgan Library. The same samples hung in the smudged front window for all the years I shopped there. The same ladies, quiet and gently dotty, were there every time I popped in. The light was dim, and the sum total of the creature comforts consisted of two folding chairs in front of the window. Adding to the shop's fascination were rumors that the women who worked there were more like characters from *Bell, Book, and Candle* than one might expect to meet at your a run-of-the-mill LYS.

I hope they were! I miss them so much. I miss their complete range of Rowan yarns, stacked to the ceiling on

Reader, I made that sweater.

All of this was new to me. *Terra incognita.* I was enchanted.

After a quick session on someone else's needles to see if I remembered to knit from a dubious pair of slippers I'd made as a Camp Fire Girl twenty years earlier (I did remember), I left the shop with an armful of bulky hand-dyed red/pink merino and instructions for a sweater jotted on a single sheet of paper.

Reader, I made that sweater. It was the start of a love that, twenty-five years later, has never flickered, and in fact blazes brighter all the time.

In those pre-internet (by which I mean pre-knitting blogs! Pre-Ravelry! Pre-Instagram!) days, a New York City knitter got her yarn by almost furtive, feral means. We knitters haunted cramped second-story shops that were presided

metal shelving. I miss pawing through their flat stacks of books. I miss their kind advice to me on how to do things more easily. I even miss their arched eyebrows when I dared to enter with a young child in tow.

Yes, yarn stores are better now, even in New York's crazy real estate market. They are friendlier. They are better lit, and they are even more stuffed with good yarns than before. But I miss the days when being a knitter in New York meant climbing creaking stairs, and possibly encountering a coven.

The Northern half of Mason-Dixon Knitting, Kay Gardiner has been a Knit Yorker for decades, which is amazing considering her youth and charm. She has shared her fibery obsession for years with Southerner Ann Shayne, but adventures with second-story LYSes came first.

Meet the Yarn

Alice O'Reilly
Backyard Fiberworks

The perception of color is one of the most personal things a human can experience. It's not the rods and cones and whatever brain juice makes your eyes see things, but rather the emotional reaction to color that makes it all your own. Color can trigger feelings and moods. It can take you back to places you've been or flavors you've savored. Color is a Proustian madeleine full of memory and meaning. To react to that memory and that feeling is the most critical part of color theory, to my mind, and one that's often overlooked. Something that starts with our eyes but goes straight to our lizard brain, something so profound you can feel it.

The same experimentation, reaction, and evaluation, exist when "designing" new colors. Starting with a color concept is usually the beginning, knowing that you'd like a certain kind of blue or a certain tone or saturation. The tinkering begins, with mason jars full of dye and paper towels soaked with variations on the theme, until inspiration strikes, and you feel it. The One.

Any creative undertaking requires a certain leap of faith. Faith not necessarily in your abilities as a knitter, or a

crafter, or a creative person, but rather faith in possibility. This "faith-based crafting" idea permeates the exploration of color and encourages you to be available to possibility. You don't know how to get there yet because each new color is a new exploration, bringing elements together in a way you have not seen before. You can experiment and engage with the process, and suddenly you have this color that evokes a feeling. That, when you hold it in your hands, reminds you of summer, or snow, or whole wheat toast, or *something* that makes it feel right.

And the thing to remember about color theory at Backyard Fiberworks is that this feeling is always true. Because *you* see it like no one else, even when we look at the exact same colors. You know what works for you and that color confidence rings true because, when a color clicks into place, it is a physical reaction. You can feel the tension resolve, the colors slide into place next to their partners, and the expression is complete.

When color and fiber are bonded through the alchemic magic of dyeing, the result is a spellbinding synthesis that will make your heart leap. Each yarn takes dye a little differently, as each breed of sheep, shade of fiber, or twist and ply has a personality and a way of reflecting that color back to you all its own. Superwash fibers are thirsty for dye and soak it up in the blink of an eye, which can create beautiful speckles when the dye strikes in an instant. Silk is a more stubborn creature, less inclined to be dyed without effort, but wow—when it does, you want to be there. Wool is not as monolithic as its single name would suggest, and each breed and fiber has a unique construction and temperament. Understanding how the yarn was spun and plied, as well as which fibers it is made from, can give you great insight into how it will behave both in the dyepot and on the needles.

All of the yarns used in **I Knit New York** have unique features and qualities that make them good choices for their associated patterns. The following is a quick trip through the yarns, with descriptions of their most defining attributes, to help identify what makes them special.

Homestead

3-ply Aran weight
181 yards/100 grams
80% merino/10% nylon/10% cashmere

Homestead is an unapologetic pile of fluff in the skein, just lying there looking squishy and soft. But when it is time to make some cables really pop, this yarn is the one you want. The **Opal Clock** shawl is knit in Homestead and the combination of pattern and yarn is especially appealing, as it showcases your crisp stitches while still irresistibly calling for you to touch it and admire the downy goodness.

Meadow

4-ply DK weight
231 yards/100 grams
80% merino/10% nylon/10% cashmere

While yarn made of cashmere might be perceived as a delicate prima donna, Meadow is the hard-working luxurious yarn that you can count on to also be sturdy enough for lace work and cables. It's got stitch definition for days, and a little secret about Meadow is that it accommodates a variety of gauges like a boss, easily traversing from sport to DK to worsted weight. The **Brooklyn Botanic** beanie calls for Meadow, which is the perfect choice to make warm, soft hats for any wearer.

Meadow Light

2-ply fingering weight
435 yards/100 grams
80% merino/10% nylon/10% cashmere

A lighter weight of the fan-favorite Meadow, Meadow Light knits up into a sumptuous lofty fabric. This is the yarn you want next to your skin, a luxury with an underlying sturdiness that makes it a good choice for gloves, hats, or a pair of special socks. Meadow Light is an excellent choice for colorwork because the smooth resulting fabric shows the patterns so clearly, whether the colors are deep jeweled hues or blushing pastels. The **Manhattanhenge** cowl and gloves set and the **Metropolitan Opera** hat are knit with Meadow Light, and the resulting colorwork is crisp and defined without losing any of that cashmere coziness.

Prairie

Single-ply fingering weight
400 yards/100 grams
100% superwash merino

Prairie will win you over with its earnestness—a single-ply, nothing complicated. The cozy texture produces a fabric with a subtle plush halo that evokes a rustic simplicity, while the saturated colors glow with the vibrancy and movement of wheat fields. Both the **Jane Jacobs** shawl and the **Sheep Meadow** cowl are knit in Prairie, where the designer's use of texture and color showcase the yarn beautifully.

Terrain

3-ply sport weight
328 yds/100 grams
100% superwash merino

Bouncy and cheerful, Terrain's 3-ply structure creates a rounded smooth yarn with beautiful stitch definition and a fabric resistant to pilling. This structural building block wears well but still feels good as it flows through your hands. The **Rockefeller Center** top, **Go Lightly** pullover, and **42nd & Lex** cardigan are all knit in Terrain, as the weight is perfect for lighter sweaters.

Tundra

Single-ply super bulky weight
78 yards/100 grams
80% superwash merino/20% nylon

Tundra is for when you want to go big (not go home). This yarn is perfect for creating cozy accessories, and the single-ply texture adds to the lush and welcoming feel. If you want the satisfaction of a fast project, bulky is where it's at. The **Lenox Avenue** hat is a quick knit with Tundra that shows off the yarn's touchable texture in chunky cables.

42nd & Lex

Kathleen Dames

Do you know the corner of 42nd Street and Lexington Avenue? It's one of those magical Manhattan intersections with the Chanin Building on one corner, the Marketplace side of Grand Central Terminal on another, and then, the jewel in the crown of the Manhattan skyline, the Chrysler Building on the northeast corner. Does a building, a midtown office tower, get any more magical? Not to me. So, when I looked at a lily-of-the-valley pattern variation one day, I saw it! With some adjustments, there was the unmistakeable top of everyone's favorite New York skyscraper.

This cardigan's unique construction begins with the sleeves and yoke worked from cuff to center back, which are woven together, then the skirt is knit separately, which allows you to have all those lace elements facing the right direction in the right places. With open fronts and the feel of a shrug, you'll throw this sweater over everything.

Sizes
XS (S, M, L, 1X, 2X, 3X) shown in size XS with zero ease

Finished Measurements
Bust: 32 (36, 40, 44, 48, 52, 56) inches/81.5 (91.5, 101.5, 112, 122, 132, 142) cm

Materials
Backyard Fiberworks Terrain (100% superwash merino; 328 yd/316 m per 3.5 oz/100 g skein);
  color: Dove; 3 (3, 4, 4, 5, 6, 6) skeins
US5/3.75 mm 29-inch/75-cm circular needle + set of DPNs (or size needed to achieve gauge)
Stitch markers, waste yarn or stitch holders, tapestry needle

Gauge
21 sts x 24 rows = 3 inches/7.5 cm in Chrysler Lace, after blocking
24 sts x 30 rows = 4 inches/10 cm in Stockinette Stitch, after blocking

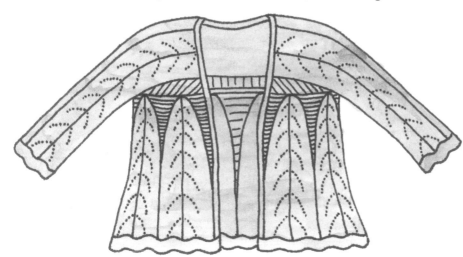

finished bust
  32 (36. 40, 44, 48, 52, 56) inches
  81 (91.5, 101.5, 112, 122, 132, 142) cm
shoulder width
  4 ½ (4 ¾, 5, 5, 5 ¼, 5 ½, 5 ¾) inches
  11.5 (12, 12.5, 13, 13.5, 14, 14.5) cm
¾-sleeve length
  15 (15 ½, 16, 16 ½, 17, 17 ½, 18) inches
  38 (39.5, 40.5, 42, 43, 44.5, 45.5) cm
back of neck width
  3 (3 ½, 4, 4 ½, 5, 5 ½, 6) inches
  7.5 (9, 10, 11.5, 12.5, 14, 15) cm
body length
  12 ½ (12 ½, 14, 14, 14, 15 ½, 15 ½) inches
  32 (32, 35.5, 35.5, 35.5, 39.5, 39.5) cm

NOTES

- Sweater begins with left sleeve cuff worked back-and-forth and the remainder of the sleeve worked in-the-round, switches to being worked back-and-forth and proceeds to left shoulder/yoke, then left back; stitches are held for joining. Right sleeve begins as for left, then proceeds to right shoulder, yoke, and back. After weaving together the back, the sleeves and yoke (now one piece) are set aside for the body, which is worked back-and-forth from the bottom-up in one piece. Finally, the body is sewn to the lower edge of the yoke.
- While the sweater is shown with ¾ sleeves and a hip-length body, you can customize your cardigan with longer sleeves (work more Chrysler Lace repeats before Shoulder Section) or a thigh-grazing skirt (more repeats of Chrysler Lace and/or plain rows after Chrysler Tower Chart).

PATTERN

Sleeves

Make two. Follow Left side instructions for first sleeve, then Right side instructions for second.

With DPNs CO 60 (70, 74, 82, 86, 90, 94) sts. Distribute sts

evenly over 4 DPNs and work with fifth. Work back and forth in Garter Stitch for 10 rows. Join for working in the round and pl m to indicate BOR.

Set-up rnd: P4 (6, 7, 9, 10, 11, 13) sts, pl m, work first rnd of Chrysler Lace over 22 sts, pl m, p7 (11, 15, 17, 20, 23, 24) sts, pl m, work first rnd of Chrysler Lace over 21 sts, pl m, p5 (7, 8, 10, 11, 12, 14) sts.

Maintaining Reverse Stockinette Stitch and Chrysler Lace panels, work even until sleeve measures 15 (15 ½, 16, 16 ½, 17, 17 ½, 18) inches or desired length to underarm, ending with an even row.

Shoulder Section

Switch to working back-and-forth, working even chart rows as RS rows. Work in est patts until yoke measures 6 (6 ½, 6 ¾, 7, 7 ½, 8, 8 ¼) inches from switch point, ending on the RS for the Left Sleeve and the WS for the Right Sleeve. Make note of last row of Chrysler Lace worked. *You will now create the Garter Stitch Collar Edge then attach it perpendicularly to the yoke sts every other row.*

Left Collar Edge	Right Collar Edge
At end of last RS row CO 5 sts—65 (75, 79, 87, 91, 95, 99) sts.	At end of last WS row CO 5 sts—65 (75, 79, 87, 91, 95, 99) sts.
WS: Sl1 p-wise wyif then bring yarn to back between ndls, k3, p2tog—1 st dec'd. Turn.	*RS:* Sl1 p-wise wyif then bring yarn to back between ndls, k3, k2tog-b—1 st dec'd. Turn.
RS: Sl1 k-wise wyib, k4. Turn.	*WS:* Sl1 k-wise wyif, k4. Turn.

Work these two rows for Left or Right Collar Edge 30 (34, 37, 40, 43, 45, 47) times total—35 (39, 42, 45, 48, 50, 52) sts. *You will now attach the Garter Stitch Edge to the upper back edge of the yoke to begin the back of the collar.*

Top of Left Collar Edge (RS):	Top of Right Collar Edge (RS):
Work 25 (30, 32, 36, 38, 40, 42) sts, pl m, k4, k2tog-b (last st of back with first st of edge). Turn.	On last row, sl1, k3, k2tog-b, k4, pl m, work in est patts to end of row.
WS: Sl1 k-wise, k4, sl m, work to end of row.	*WS:* Work to m, sl m, k4, p2tog. Turn.
RS: Work to m, sl m, k4, k2tog-b. Turn.	*RS:* Sl1 k-wise wyib, work to end of row.

Work these two rows for for Left or Right Collar Edge 10 rows total—30 (35, 37, 41, 43, 45, 47) sts.

Center Back

Slipping the first st of the Collar Edge p-wise (WS for Left Sleeve, RS for Right Sleeve), k4, work in established patterns to end of row. Continue working back-and-forth on remaining sts for 2 (2, 2, 3, 3, 3, 3) repeats of Chrysler Lace ending with row 12.

For Left Sleeve place sts on waste yarn or stitch holder, break yarn, and set aside.

For Right Sleeve keep sts live on ndl at end of Center Back.

Chrysler Tower

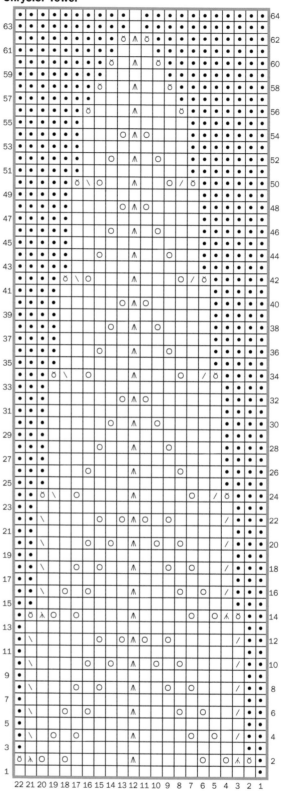

Finish Center Back

Slip Left side sts to second ndl and with 18-inch piece of working yarn and tapestry needle graft center back sts together using Kitchener Stitch for Reverse Stockinette, Stockinette (for Chrysler Lace), and Garter as appropriate (see Techniques, p. 67).

Body

With circular ndl CO 187 (209, 231, 253, 275, 297, 319) sts.
Slipping first st of every row p-wise wyif then bringing yarn to back, work back-and-forth in Garter stitch for 11 rows.
Setup Row (WS): Sl1, k4, pl m, work row 1 of Chrysler Lace 8 (9, 10, 11, 12, 13, 14) times total, k1, pl m, k5.
Continue in established patterns for 3 (3, 4, 4, 4, 5, 5) vertical repeats of Chrysler Lace. Switch to Chrysler Tower and work 64 rows. BO all sts.

FINISHING

With RS facing attach top of body to lower edge of yoke/ back evenly with mattress stitch using tapestry needle and 18-inch lengths of working yarn (longer pieces of yarn tend to get tangled). Match up front edges of both pieces as well as center back grafting line with center of body piece. Seam up Garter Stitch cuffs. Weave in all ends. Block to finished measurements.

Chrysler Lace

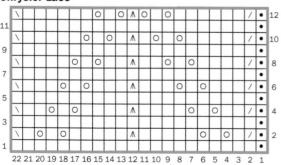

Chart Key

☐ = knit	• = purl
╱ = k2tog	○ = yarnover
⋀ = s2kpo	╲ = ssk
⋀ = k3tog	λ = sk2p
ᕤ = m1-L	☐ = repeat

Brooklyn Botanic

Brittney Bailey

Established in 1910 and situated on fifty-two acres in the heart of Brooklyn, the Brooklyn Botanic Garden is one of the most magical, breathtaking spaces in the city. With rolling landscapes and rare flora and fauna housed in charming art nouveau greenhouses, the garden is an escape from the big city, while also very "New York."

The Brooklyn Botanic beanie allows you to take that charming combination of nature and nouveau with you everywhere you go! The eyelet ribbing, inspired by the greenhouse architecture, supports a beautiful floral lace pattern that is suggestive of the rich (almost overwhelming, but not quite) plant life of the Brooklyn Botanic Garden!

Sizes
S (M, L) shown in size S

Finished Measurements
Circumference: To fit head circumference of 19 ½, (21 ½, 23) inches/49.5 (54.5, 58.5) cm when stretched
Length: 9¼ inches/23.5 cm or 11 inches/28 cm for slouchier hat

Materials
Backyard Fiberworks Meadow (80% merino, 10% nylon, 10% cashmere; 231 yds/211 m per 3.5 oz/100 g skein);
   color: Plume; 1 (1, 2) skeins
US4/3.5 mm 16-inch/40-cm circular needle (or one size smaller than gauge needle)
US5/3.75 mm 16-inch/40-cm circular needle + set of DPNs for crown shaping (or size needed to achieve gauge)
Stitch marker, tapestry needle

Gauge
24 sts x 32 rnds over 4 inches/10 cm in Stockinette Stitch with larger needle, after blocking
28 sts x 40 rnds over 4 inches/10 cm in Floral Lace with larger needle, after blocking

PATTERN

Hat Brim

With smaller ndl CO 110 (125, 140) sts and join for working in the rnd.

Rnd 1: *K3, p2; repeat from * to end of rnd.

Rnd 2: *K1, yo, k2tog, p2; repeat from * to end of rnd.

Rnd 3: Repeat rnd 1.

Rnd 4: *K2tog, yo, k1, p2; repeat from * to end of rnd.

Repeat rnds 1–4 until work measures 1½ inches/4cm from CO and ending with either rnd 1 or rnd 3.

Next Rnd: Change to larger ndl, *k55 (41, 35), m1; repeat from * to last 0 (2, 0) sts, k0 (2, 0)— 112, (128, 144) sts.

Hat Body

Repeat Floral Lace rnds 1–12 three times (four times for a slouchier fit) total, then work rnds 1–3 once more.

Next Rnd: Knit to end of rnd.

Crown

Change to DPNs when sts no longer fit comfortably around ndl.

Rnd 13: (K14, skp) around—105 (120, 135) sts.

Rnd 14 (and all even rnds): Knit to end of rnd.

Rnd 15: (K13, skp) around—98 (112, 126) sts.

Rnd 17: (K12, skp) around—91 (104, 117) sts.

Rnd 19: (K11, skp) around—84 (96, 108) sts.

Rnd 21: (K10, skp) around—77 (88, 99) sts.

Rnd 23: (K8, sk2p) around—63 (72, 81) sts.

Rnd 25: (K6, sk2p) around—49 (56, 63) sts.

Rnd 27: (K4, sk2p) around—35 (40, 45) sts.

Rnd 29: (K2, sk2p) around—21 (24, 27) sts.

Rnd 31: *K2tog; repeat to last 3 (6, 9) sts, sk2p 1 (2, 3) times—10 (11, 12) sts.

FINISHING

Break yarn, thread with darning needle and pull needle through remaining live sts and pull tight to secure top. Turning work inside out weave in this end and all other ends. Block gently and enjoy!

Floral Lace

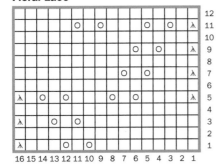

Chart Key

☐ = knit

Ⓞ = yarnover

Ⲗ = sk2p

■ = repeat

Floral Lace Instructions

Rnd 1: *K9, yo, k1, yo, k3, sk2p; repeat from * to end.

Rnd 2 and all even numbered rnds: Knit to end of rnd.

Rnd 3: *K10, yo, k1, yo, k2, sk2p; repeat from * to end of rnd.

Rnd 5: *K3tog, k4, yo, k1, yo, k3, (yo, k1) twice, sk2p; repeat from * to end of rnd.

Rnd 7: *K3tog, k3, yo, k1, yo, k9; repeat from * to end of rnd.

Rnd 9: *K3tog, (k1, yo) twice, k3, yo, k1, yo, k4, sk2p; repeat from * to end of rnd.

Rnd 11: *K3tog, (k1, yo) twice, k3, yo, k1, yo, k4, sk2p; repeat to end of rnd.

Rnd 12: Knit to end of rnd.

One belongs to New York instantly, one belongs to it as much in five minutes as in five years.

—*Tom Wolfe*

Go Lightly

Brittney Bailey

Inspired by Audrey Hepburn's iconic style in Breakfast At Tiffany's, the "Go Lightly" pullover is a timeless combination of comfort and chic. Casting on at the top, the collar features a folded hem that creates a unique and stylish boatneck. The little bit of eyelet detail along the raglan increases and down the side seams adds a delicate feminine touch making it perfect for visits to Sing Sing, while the relaxed fit gives the sweater an "Audrey Off-Duty" feel that will have you singing "Moon River" all day long.

Sizes

S (M, L, XL, 2X, 3X) shown in size S with 3 inches/7.5 cm positive ease

Finished Measurements

Bust: 35 (38, 41, 44, 47, 50) inches/89 (96.5, 104, 112, 119.5, 127) cm

Material

Backyard Fiberworks Terrain (100% superwash merino; 328 yd/316 m per 3.5 oz/100 g skein); color: Ume; 3 (4, 4, 4, 5, 5) skeins
US3/3.25 mm 16-inch/40-cm circular needle + 24-inch/60-cm circular needle + set of DPNs for sleeves
   (or size needed to achieve gauge)
8–10 stitch markers, tapestry needle

Gauge

28 sts x 36 rnds = 4 inches/10 cm in Stockinette Stitch, after blocking

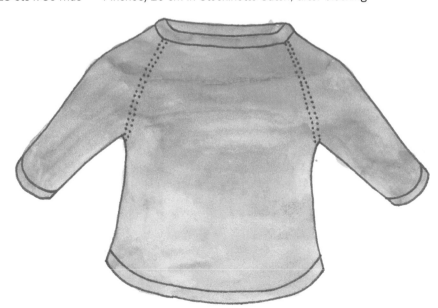

finished bust
   35 (38, 41, 44, 47, 50) inches
   89 (96.5, 104, 112, 119.5, 127) cm
collar
   24 (24 ¼, 24 ¾, 24 ¾, 26 ¼, 26 ½) inches
   61 (61.5, 63, 63, 66.5, 67.5) cm
¾-sleeve length (from underarm)
   9 ¼ (9 ½, 9 ½, 9 ¾, 9 ¾, 10) inches
   23.5 (24, 24, 24.5, 24.5, 25.5) cm
body length (from underarm)
   12 (12 ¼, 12 ½, 12 ¾, 13, 13 ¼) inches
   30.5 (31.5, 32, 32.5, 33, 34) cm

PATTERN

Collar

Using shorter circular ndl, CO 168 (170, 174, 176, 184, 186) sts, pl m to indicate BOR, and join for working in the rnd being careful not to twist stitches.

Collar Rnd 1: Knit to end of rnd.

Repeat rnd 1 twelve times more.

Collar Rnd 2: Purl to end of rnd.

Collar Rnd 3: Knit to end of rnd.

Repeat rnd 3 eleven times more.

Next rnd: Fold work in half so that CO edge aligns with current rnd. With the right ndl pick up first CO stitch and knit it together with first stitch on the left ndl, continue in this manner until all sts in the rnd have been worked.

Raglan setup

K62 (65, 67, 69, 74, 75) back sts, pl m, k2, pl m, k18 (16, 16, 14, 14, 14) left sleeve sts, pl m, k2, pl m, k62 (65, 67, 69, 74, 75) front sts, pl m, k2, pl m, k18 (16, 16, 14, 14, 14) left sleeve sts, pl m, k2.

Raglan Rnd 1 (Increase rnd): *K1, m1-L, knit to 1 st before m,

m1-R, k1, sl m, k2, sl m, k1, m1-L, knit to 1 st before m, m1-R, k1, sl m, k2, sl m; repeat from * to end of rnd—8 sts inc'd; 176 (178, 182, 182, 192, 194) sts.

Raglan Rnd 2: Knit to end of rnd, sl m's as you come to them.

Raglan Rnd 3 (Increase rnd): *K1, m1-L, knit to 1 st before m, m1-R, k1, sl m, yo, k2tog, sl m, k1, m1-L, knit to 1 st before m, m1-R, k1, sl m, k2tog, yo, sl m; repeat from * to end of rnd—8 sts inc'd.

Switch to longer circular ndl when sts will comfortably fit.

Repeat rnds 2 & 3 six times, then only rnd 2 once more—232 (234, 238, 238, 248, 250) sts.

Short rows

Short Row 1: K1, m1-L, knit to 4 sts before m, w+t.

Short Row 2: Purl to 5 sts before BOR m, w+t.

Short Row 3: Knit to 3 sts before previously wrapped stitch, w+t.

Short Row 4: Purl to 3 sts before previously wrapped stitch, w+t.

Repeat short rows 3 & 4 six times more.

You will now return to knitting in the rnd and complete rnd as follows: Knit to 1 st before m working wrapped sts as you come to them, m1-R, k1, sl m, yo, k2tog, sl m, k1, m1-L, knit to 1 st before m, m1-R, k1, sl m, k2tog, yo, sl m; repeat from * to end of rnd—240 (242, 246, 246, 256, 258) sts.

Repeat Raglan Rnds 2 & 3 until you have 376 (410, 446, 478, 512, 554) sts—114 (125, 135, 145, 156, 167) sts for front and back and 70 (76, 84, 90, 96, 106) sts for each sleeve + 8 eyelet sts.

Repeat Raglan Rnd 2 once more.

Raglan Rnd 4: *Knit to m, sl m, yo, k2tog, sl m, k to m, sl m, k2tog, yo; repeat from * once more—no stitches increased.

Repeat Raglan Rnds 2 & 4, maintaining eyelets, but with no further increases until front of work measures 7 ½ (8 ¼, 8 ¾, 9 ¼, 10, 10 ½) inches/19 (21, 22, 23.5, 25.5, 26.5) cm from the start of raglan increases.

Note: be careful not to measure from the back, as the extra length created by the short rows will throw off the measurement.

Divide for Sleeves

Knit to m, remove m, k2, pl next 70 (76, 84, 90, 96, 106) sts on holder or waste yarn, CO 2 sts, pl m to indicate side seam, CO 2 more sts (4 underarm sts total), k2, remove next m, knit to m, remove m, k2, pl next 70 (76, 84, 90, 96, 106) sts on holder or waste yarn, CO 2 sts, pl m (new BOR m), CO 2 stitches more (4 underarm stitches total), k2, remove m—244 (266, 286, 306, 328, 350) sts total for body.

Body

Body Rnd 1: Knit to end of rnd.

Body Rnd 2: Knit to m, sl m, k2tog, yo, knit to 2 sts before m, yo, k2tog.

Repeat Body Rnds 1 & 2 until work measures 10 ½ (10 ¾, 11, 11 ¼, 11 ½, 11 ¾) inches/26.5 (27.5, 28, 28.5, 29, 30) cm from underarm, or to approximately 1 ½ inches/4 cm less than desired length.

Continue with no further decreases until sleeve measures 8 ¼ (8 ½, 8 ½, 8 ¾, 8 ¾, 9) inches/21 (21.5, 21.5, 22, 22, 23) cm from underarm or to 1 inch/2.5 cm less than desired length.

Cuff
Rnd 3: (K1, p1) around.
Repeat this rnd until cuff measures 1 inch.
BO loosely in pattern.

FINISHING
Weave in all ends. Block to finished measurements.

Brittney Loves NY

What has your knitwear design journey been like?
Scary and fun! I've met some incredible people and made some amazing friends through the process of knitwear design. I still consider myself to be a novice in many ways, but each new pattern I create teaches me something new about my craft. It's completely addictive.

Tell us a brush with fame New York story.
Oh gosh, I have had so many thanks to my work at Purl Soho. I've gotten the chance to help a fair few celebrities shop for yarn which has been fun, but I did lose my head a bit on the morning that I passed Justin Timberlake, Jessica Biel, and their family crossing Canal Street on my way to work.

Subway knitting: must-have or never ever?
Yes always to subway knitting, but the trick is to stick to stockinette/garter stitch as much as possible!

Picker or thrower? Project monogamy or cast on all the things?
Thrower, essentially project monogamy, but sometimes I cheat.

Favorite places to eat/drink/knit in NYC?
I love to knit in Washington Square Park (I haven't lived in NYC that long, so I still get to be a tourist sometimes) and Double Dutch Espresso in Harlem.

Movies

1. *Breakfast at Tiffany's* (big surprise there)
2. *On the Town*
3. *Barefoot in the Park*
4. *Manhattan*
5. *You've Got Mail*
6. *Tootsie*
7. *When Harry Met Sally*
8. *Annie Hall*
9. *Muppets Take Manhattan*
10. *Serendipity*

Repeat Body Rnd 1 (knitting all sts) for 14 rnds.
Next Rnd: Purl to end of rnd.
Next Rnd: Repeat rnd 1 (knitting all sts) for 14 more rnds.

Folded Hem
Fold work over at purl rnd, pick up purl bump 14 rnds prior to the first stitch in the rnd (where the fabric should naturally fall) and knit together with first st on the ndo, repeat as established knitting all live sts to corresponding purl bump, until all sts have been worked. BO loosely.

Sleeves
Transfer all sts from waste yarn or holder to DPNs and pick up 4 sts from underarm—74 (80, 88, 94, 100, 110) sts. Pl BOR m at the center of underarm.
Sleeve Rnd 1: Knit to end of rnd.
Sleeve Rnd 2 (decrease rnd): K1, ssk, knit to three sts before end of rnd, k2tog, k1
Repeat Sleeve Rnd 2 every 10 (8, 6, 6, 5, 4)th rnd 6 (8, 12, 13, 14, 18) times more—60 (62, 64, 68, 70, 72) sts.

Jane Jacobs

Kirsten Kapur

This asymmetrical mosaic shawl is named for Jane Jacobs, a community activist who led the charge to protect Washington Square Park from Robert Moses's "urban renewal" project. Under his plan 5th Avenue would have been extended through the park, destroying the beloved space we know today.

Jane Jacobs begins with only a few stitches and increases in width to form its easy-to-wear shape. Although this is a shawl, it is important to obtain gauge in order to avoid running out of yarn. Adjust needle size as necessary to obtain gauge. The gauge given in the pattern is a blocked gauge. This shawl is worked flat, however a circular needle is used to hold the large number of stitches. If desired, straight needles may be used to start.

Sizes
One Size

Finished Measurements
Width across top edge: 70 inches/178 cm
Depth from top edge to point: 28 ½ inches/72 cm

Materials
Backyard FIberworks Prairie (100% superwash merino; 400 yds/366 m per 3.5 oz/100 g skein)
    Color A: Rainwater; 1 skein
    Color B: Pollen; 1 skein
    Color C: Deep Creek; 1 skein
US6/4mm 32-inch/81-cm circular needle (or size needed to achieve gauge)
Tapestry needle, stitch markers

Gauge
17 sts x 34 rows = 4 inches/10 cm in Garter Stitch, after blocking

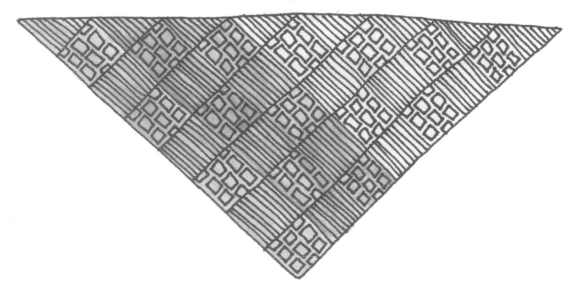

NOTES

- Each right side row increases the overall stitch count by 1 stitch.
- Placements 1 and 2 are alternated throughout. Each placement is worked for 48 rows, and increases the overall stitch count by 24 stitches.
- Colors are alternated every two rows throughout the pattern. It is not necessary to carry two yarns on each row. Slipped stitches create the patterning.
- When alternating colors every two rows it is not necessary to cut the yarn. Simply carry them up the side by bringing the new color up from behind the old color. Keep these carries loose to allow the edge to block fully.
- Since the sequence of the colors changes throughout the pattern, the color positions are listed as Color 1 and Color 2 for the Squares Pattern. Each section will define which color to use in position 1 and which to use in position 2.
- At the first row of sections 2–8, a yarn over is followed by two slipped stitches. Be sure to maintain the placement of this yarn over, and work the yarn over as a separate stitch on the following row, where it will come after the two slipped stitches.
- The edges will look a little uneven between sections as you work. This is normal since slipped stitches tend to pull the work in a bit more. This will even out with blocking. However, it is important to keep the floats behind the slipped stitches loose in order to avoid too much puckering and to match the garter stitch gauge as closely as possible.

Schematic Notes

- This schematic shows the position of the Squares Pattern in each section. The other sections are garter stitch stripes.
- The edge stitches are not shown in this schematic.
- One yarn over increase is worked 2 stitches in from the

beginning of each right side row. See pattern instructions for more information.

- The Squares sections each have 26 stitches. The stockinette stripes sections each have 22 stitches. The triangle at the beginning of each section has 3 stitches after working row 1, increasing by 1 stitch on every right side row, ending with 26 stitches. Markers are moved for each section, see Placement 1 and Placement 2 for more information.

70"/178cm

Section 8 Placement 2
Section 7 Placement 1
Section 6 Placement 2
Section 5 Placement 1
Section 4 Placement 2
Section 3 Placement 1
Section 2 Establish Pattern
Section 1 Set Up

28½"/72cm

Squares
Squares
Squares
Squares
Squares
Squares
Squares

Squares
Squares
Squares
Squares
Squares

Squares
Squares
Squares

Squares

Placement 1

Note: Work rows 1–24 of the Squares Pattern in sequence. Alternate colors every two rows. The color placements vary throughout the pattern. See instructions for each section for color placement.

Row 1 (RS): K2, yo, pl m, *work the next 26 sts in Squares Pattern, pl m, k22, pl m; repeat from * to last 4 sts, k4.

Row 2 (WS): K4, *sl m, knit to m, sl m, work in Squares Pattern to m; repeat from * to last m, sl m, knit to end.

Row 3: K2, yo, knit to m, sl m, *work to m in Squares Pattern, sl m, knit to m, sl m; repeat from * to last 4 sts, k4.

Row 4: Repeat Row 2.

Continue working as established in Rows 3 & 4, working each row of Squares Pattern in sequence and alternating colors every two rows. Work rows 1–24 of the Squares Pattern twice for a total of 48 rows. Remove markers on last row.

Placement 2

Note: Work rows 1–24 of the Squares Pattern in sequence. Alternate colors every two rows. The color placements vary throughout the pattern. See instructions in each section for color placement.

Row 1 (RS): K2, yo, pl m, *work the next 26 sts in Squares Pattern, pl m, k22, pl m; repeat from * to last 28 sts, work the next 26 sts in Squares Pattern, pl m, k2.

Row 2 (WS): K2, sl m, work in Squares Pattern to next m, *slm, knit to m, sl m, work in Squares Pattern to m; repeat from * to last m, sl m, knit to end.

Row 3: K2, yo, knit to m, sl m, *work the next 26 sts in Squares Pattern, sl m, k22, sl m; repeat from * to last 28 sts, work the next 26 sts in Squares Pattern, sl m, k2.

Row 4: Repeat Row 2.

Continue working as established in Rows 3 & 4, working each row of Squares Pattern in sequence and alternating colors every two rows. Work Rows 1–24 of the Squares Pattern twice for a total of 48 rows. Remove markers on the last row.

Squares Pattern

Chart Key

- ▨ = Color position 1
- ☐ = Color position 2
- ☐ = RS: knit, WS: purl
- ⊡ = RS: purl, WS: knit
- ⊙ = yarnover
- ⊻ = RS: sl wyib, WS: sl wyif
- ☐ = repeat

Squares Pattern Notes

- The repeat section is worked 3 times — this is the section in the red box on the chart, and the stitches that follow the * in the written Squares Pattern.
- Colors are alternated every two rows throughout. The column to the right of the chart is for color placement and should not be worked.
- Color positions change throughout the pattern. These positions are represented by Color 1 and Color 2 for the chart and written version of the Squares Pattern.
  For sections 2–5 Color 1 = Color B and Color 2 = Color A.
  For sections 5–7 Color 1 = Color B and Color 2 = Color C.
  For section 8 Color 1 = Color A and Color 2 = Color C.

Squares Pattern Instructions

Row 1 (RS): With Color 1, *sl2 wyib, k6; repeat from * three times, sl2 wyib.

Row 2 (WS): With Color 1, sl2 wyif, *k6, sl2 wyif; repeat from * three times.

Row 3: With Color 2, *(k2, sl2 wyib) twice; repeat from * three times, k2.

Row 4: With Color 2, k2, *(sl2 wyif, k2) twice; repeat from * three times.

Row 5: With Color 1, *(sl2 wyib, k2) twice; repeat from * three times, sl2 wyib.

Row 6: With Color 1, sl2 wyif, *(k2, sl2 wyif) twice; repeat from * three times.

Row 7: With Color 2, repeat Row 3.

Row 8: With Color 2, repeat Row 4.

Row 9: With Color 1, repeat Row 1.

Row 10: With Color 1, repeat Row 2.

Rows 11–12: With Color 2, knit.

Row 13: With Color 1, *k4, sl2 wyib, k2; repeat from * three times, k2.

Row 14: With Color 1, k2, *k2, sl2 wyif, k4; repeat from * three times.

Row 15: With Color 2, repeat Row 3.

Row 16: With Color 2, repeat Row 4.

Row 17: With Color 1, repeat Row 5.

Row 18: With Color 1, repeat Row 6.

Row 19: With Color 2, repeat Row 3.

Row 20: With Color 2, repeat Row 4.

Row 21: With Color 1, repeat Row 13.

Row 22: With Color 1, repeat Row 14.

Rows 23–24: With Color 2, knit.

PATTERN

Set Up—Section 1
With Color A, CO 4 sts.
Row 1 (WS): With Color A, knit.
Row 2 (RS): With Color B, k2, yo, knit to end—1 st inc'd.
Row 3: With Color B, knit.
Row 4: With Color A, k2, yo, knit to end—1 st inc'd.
Row 5: With Color A, knit.
Repeat Rows 2–5 twelve more times—30 sts.

Establish Pattern—Section 2
Note: Work rows 1–24 of the Squares Pattern in sequence. Alternate Colors B and A every two rows throughout. Use Color B in the Color 1 position, and Color A in the Color 2 position of the squares pattern.
Row 1 (RS): K2, yo, pl m, work the next 26 sts in Squares Pattern (see notes), pl m, k2—1 st inc'd.
Row 2 (WS): K2, sl m, work in Squares Pattern to next m, sl m, knit to end.
Row 3: K2, yo, knit to m, sl m, work in Squares Pattern to next m, sl m, k2—1 st inc'd.
Row 4: Repeat Row 2.
Continue working as established in Rows 3 & 4, working each row of Squares Pattern in sequence and alternating colors every two rows. Work Rows 1–24 of the Squares Pattern twice for a total of 48 rows.

Section 3
Beginning with Color B, work as instructed in Placement 1 (see box), alternating Colors B and A every two rows throughout.
Use Color B in the Color 1 position, and Color A in the Color 2 position of the Squares Pattern—78 sts.

Section 4
Beginning with Color B, work as instructed in Placement 2 (see box), alternating Colors B and A every two rows throughout.
Use Color B in the Color 1 position, and Color A in the Color 2 position of the Squares Pattern—102 sts.

Section 5
Beginning with Color B, work as instructed in Placement 1 (see box), alternating Colors B and A every two rows throughout.
Use Color B in the Color 1 position, and Color A in the Color 2 position of the Squares Pattern.
When you get to row 47, cut Color B leaving a tail long enough to weave in.
Join Color C and work rows 47 & 48 in Color C—126 sts.

Section 6
Beginning with Color A, work as instructed in Placement 2 (see box), alternating Colors A and C every two rows throughout.
Use Color A in the Color 1 position, and Color C in the Color 2 position of the Squares Pattern—150 sts.

Section 7
Beginning with Color A, work as instructed in Placement 1 (see box), alternating Colors A and C every two rows throughout.
Use Color A in the Color 1 position, and Color C in the Color 2 position of the Squares Pattern.
When you get to row 47, cut Color A leaving a tail long enough to weave in.
Join Color B and work rows 47 & 48 in Color B—174 sts.

Section 8
Beginning with Color C, work as instructed in Placement 2 (see box), alternating Colors B and C every two rows throughout.
Use Color C in the Color 1 position, and Color B in the Color 2 position of the Squares Pattern—198 sts.
Cut Color B, leaving a tail long enough to weave in.
With C, bind off loosely as follows:
Step 1: Knit the first two sts together through the back legs of the loops.
Step 2: Transfer the stitch back onto the left ndl.
Repeat Steps 1 & 2 until all stitches have been bound off.

FINISHING
Weave in all ends. Block to measurements in schematic.

Kirsten Loves NY

Subway knitting: must-have or never ever? Picker or thrower? Project monogamy or cast on all the things? Subway knitting: must-have. Thrower. Monogamy.

Favorite station? West 4th Street, it's smelly, dirty, and often crowded, but it's the subway station nearest my first NYC apartment. That was over 30 years ago and it's pretty much the same now as it was then.

Favorite neighborhood? If I had to pick I'd say the West Village. I love the tree-lined streets with their old buildings; plus, it's loaded with charming shops and wonderful restaurants.

Places

The NYC Ferry. My favorite way to travel to/from Brooklyn for the price of a subway fare. Download the app to easily buy tickets and check schedules. The ride is an event in itself—especially if you go all the way to Rockaway Beach. There are stops at 34th Street & Pier 11 (Wall Street) in Manhattan, and all along the Queens/Brooklyn side—with stops in neighborhoods like Astoria, Long Island City, Greenpoint, Williamsburg, Dumbo, Redhook, and Rockaway Beach. Take a ride at night for a spectacular view of the city lights.

Walking the bridges. Any of them. Don't just limit yourself to the very crowded Brooklyn Bridge. Yes, it is the most iconic, and arguably the most beautiful, but the views are wonderful from the Williamsburg Bridge and the Manhattan Bridge with no crowds, and you end up in fun neighborhoods to explore.

Governors Island. Take the Governors Island Ferry ($2 round trip) and find yourself on an historic island that has been recently converted to a beautiful park. There are two forts (Castle Williams and Fort Jay), lots of nooks and crannies to relax in (find the Hammock Grove and pull out a book or your knitting). Looking to be more active? Rent a bike and ride around the island, or hike the hills to find amazing views of the New York Harbor and the Statue of Liberty. Allow at least an extra hour to enjoy oysters and a beer at Island Oyster while looking at some of the best views of lower Manhattan

The Merchant's House Museum. Step off East 4th Street and be taken back in time in this 19th-century home that has been preserved along with the furnishings of the wealthy merchant-class family that lived there from 1835 though 1933. They have a wonderful trove of 19th century textiles including many mid-19th-century dresses. If you enjoy the macabre, catch one of the spooky candlelit tours. *Time Out New York* even rated the Merchant's House as the #1 Most Haunted Place in NYC.

Brooklyn Museum/Brooklyn Botanic Garden/Prospect Park/Brooklyn Public Library. Not quite off the beaten path, but if you only think of Manhattan when you think of NYC, you're missing out. All four are situated together so you can visit one, or all four, in a single day. The Brooklyn Museum has a world class permanent collection, along with some exceptional exhibitions. The Brooklyn Botanic Garden is a stunning oasis of plants in the middle of Brooklyn. Favorites of mine are the Bonsai collection, the Rock Garden, and the Native Flora Garden.

Fort Tryon Park/The Cloisters. Take the A train to 190th Street, and you will find yourself at a beautiful park, perched high above the Hudson River. Stroll through Fort Tryon Park and enjoy the views, along with some outstanding gardens. Eventually you will find yourself at The Cloisters a branch of the Metropolitan Museum dedicated to the art, architecture, and gardens of Medieval Europe. My personal favorites are the magnificent Unicorn Tapestries and the cloister gardens.

Behind-the-Scenes Tour of the Ellis Island Hospital. Hosted by Save Ellis Island, a group dedicated to preserving parts of Ellis Island that are at risk following Hurricane Sandy, this hard-hat tour takes you through the unrestored hospital buildings. Our tour guide was well-informed and patient as we all took hundreds of photos of this haunting relic.

Van Brunt Stillhouse. Get off the NYC Ferry in Red Hook and find your way to Van Brunt Stillhouse. Take a tour (you need to schedule ahead of time), and learn how this small batch, New York City whiskey is made. Then head to the tasting room for a delicious cocktail.

Brooklyn Shoe Space/Textile Arts Center. In the learn-a-new-skill category, you can't go wrong with either of these. Both offer weekend intensives, so if you're only here for a short time you can still take a class. I have taken classes at both and have a long list of additional classes I want to take.

DeKalb Market Hall. Food vendors galore in a casual atmosphere and, remarkably, not overly crowded (for now). You will find just about any type of food you crave. A personal favorite, the arepas at *Arepa Lady*.

Eateries/drinkeries

Freud NYC is in our old neighborhood and we've gotten to know the staff there very well. We go there more than I care to admit.

Colonie on Atlantic Ave in Brooklyn.

Freek's Mill in Gowanus.

Tia Pol in Chelsea for tapas.

Momofuku Noodle Bar for Ramen on a cold winter day—go mid-afternoon for a late lunch to avoid the crowds.

Terroir Tribeca for wine and snacks.

Lenox Avenue

Lars Rains

Starting at the north end of Central Park and stretching up to the Harlem River, Lenox Avenue was the epicenter of cultural activities during the Harlem Renaissance. Originally named after the philanthropist James Lenox, the main thoroughfare that traverses the neighborhood of Harlem is now known as Malcolm X Boulevard in honor of the slain civil rights activist.

For this long cabled hat, I wanted to weave together the different threads of New York City's history—from the Harlem Renaissance to the Harlem of today—with these interlocking cables. If you ever find yourself on Malcolm X Boulevard, be sure to stop in for some delicious soul food at Sylvia's Restaurant, then go around the corner onto Dr. Martin Luther King Jr Boulevard to visit The Studio Museum in Harlem.

Sizes
One Size

Finished Measurements
Circumference: 19 inches/48 cm unstretched
Length: 16 ½ inches/42 cm to top of hat (pompom adds 5 inches/12.5 cm)

Materials
Backyard Fiberworks Tundra (80% superwash merino, 20% nylon; 76 yds/69.5 m per 3.5 oz/100 g skein); color: Hosta; 2 skeins
US13/9mm 16-inch/40-cm circular needle + set of DPNs (or size needed to achieve gauge)
Stitch marker, cable needle, tapestry needle
Alpaca pompom

Gauge
14 sts x 15 rnds = 4 inches/10 cm in
Lenox Avenue Chart/Instructions, after blocking

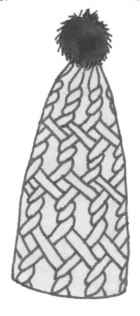

PATTERN

Body

CO 56 sts. Join for working in the rnd, being careful not to twist. Pl m to indicate BOR.

Work Rnds 1–16 of Lenox Avenue a total of three times.

Crown

Note: Switch to preferred method for small-circumference knitting when needed.

Work Rnds 17–31 of Lenox Avenue—7 sts.

Break yarn and pull through remaining 7 sts.

FINISHING

Weave in all ends with yarn needle. Block to finished measurements. Sew pompom to hat.

Lenox Avenue

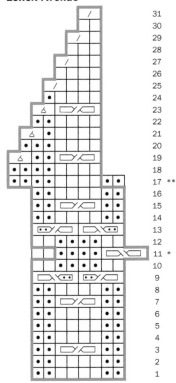

Chart Key/Stitch Instructions

☐ = knit

• = purl

▱◁▱ = C4B (Cable 4 Back): sl2 to cn to back, k2, k2 from cn

▱◁▱ = C4F (Cable 4 Front) sl2 to cn to front, k2, k2 from cn

▱•◁▱ = T4B (Twist 4 Back) sl2 to cn to back, k2, p2 from cn

▱◁•▱ = T4F (Twist 4 Front) sl2 to cn to front, p2, k2 from cn

△ = p2tog

╱ = k2tog

☐ = repeat

* Slip 2 sts, remove m, slip 2 sts back, pl m at beginning of rnd; remove m, k2, pl m at end of rnd

** Remove m, p2, pl m

Lenox Avenue Instructions

Rnd 1: (P2, k4, p2) around.

Rnd 2: Repeat Rnd 1.

Rnd 3: (P2, C4B, p2) around.

Rnds 4–6: Repeat Rnd 1.

Rnd 7: Repeat Rnd 3.

Rnd 8: Repeat Rnd 1.

Rnd 9: (T4B, T4F) around.

Rnd 10: (K2, p4, k2) to last 2 sts.

Rnd 11: Slip 2 sts, remove m, slip 2 sts back, pl m, (C4F, p4) around, remove m, k2, pl m.

Rnd 12: (K2, p4, k2) around.

Rnd 13: (T4F, T4B) around.

Rnds 14–16: Repeat Rnds 2-4.

Rnd 17: Remove m, p2, pl m, (k4, p4) around.

Rnd 18: (K4, p4) around.

Rnd 19: (C4B, p2, p2tog) around—1 st dec'd.

Rnd 20: (K4, p3) around.

Rnd 21: (K4, p1, p2tog) around—1 st dec'd.

Rnd 22: (K4, p2) around.

Rnd 23: (C4B, p2tog) around—1 st dec'd.

Rnd 24: (K4, p1) around.

Rnd 25: (K3, k2tog) around—1 st dec'd.

Rnds 26, 28, 30: Knit around.

Rnd 27: (K2, k2tog) around—1 st dec'd.

Rnd 29: (K1, k2tog) around—1 st dec'd.

Rnd 31: (K2tog) around—1 st dec'd.

Going on a #buttonhunt

Kathleen Dames

Your LYS is always a great first stop when searching for notions. But when you're in NYC, other options abound thanks to the Garment District. There are many other shops in the area that stock buttons, beads, zippers, and fabric, but here are a few I visit regularly. Almost all area shops are more than willing to take your money, even if their business is focused on wholesale. Don't forget to look up (a good rule to follow in NYC in general)! Not all shops are street-level, but don't let that dissuade you on your Garment District adventure.

P.S. I've added a couple of book stores that knitters shouldn't miss, plus a button shop away from the Garment District that is worth the trip.

Mood Designer Fabrics

225 W. 37th St., 3rd floor, Manhattan
(212) 730-5003
moodfabrics.com

If you've ever caught an episode of *Project Runway*, you know about Mood. What you may not know is that in addition to three floors of fabric, Mood is also home to a great selection of notions and trims, so it is the perfect place to scoop up some buttons for your next cardigan.

Housed in a large office building in the Garment District, visiting Mood will have you feeling like a *Project Runway* contestant or a fabulous NYC designer. While there are tourists there snapping up Mood tees, you will also find creatives comparing bolts of Belgian linen and discussing wholesale purchases with one of the black-clad assistants. This is definitely a working space for members of the garment industry.

When you enter Mood from the elevator, check your oversized bags at the door then dive into the wall of buttons in front of you. The selection leans towards fashion buttons, and I rarely leave without finding at least one good option for my project. I have been known to hem and haw for ages over half-a-dozen options laid out along the button bands of my latest design.

Buttons are displayed on the ends of their long, narrow boxes. Prices are displayed along with brief descriptions on the inside of the box lid (and a barcode for inventory management). Your challenge is to find the perfect button, then make sure there are enough in the box. Some buttons will be marked "discontinued," while others can be ordered in bulk. If you're unsure, ask one of the many friendly Mood-ies. They often have a great eye, and they know what's what in terms of their stock.

Prices range from about 25 cents for a basic shirt button to almost $20 for an all-out Swarovski-studded number, with leather toggles, brass blazer buttons, and Victorianesque glass buttons shelved alongside braided frogs and oversized decorative kilt pins. Generally buttons are boxed and shelved by category and color, so if you know you want a lightweight plastic button, you'll find a wall of choice.

While the notions corner is fantastic (feathers! fur pompoms! lace and fringe!), be sure to wander through the entire store to get the full Mood experience. Fabric-wise they stock everything from wool suiting to upholstery fabrics to silk jersey, plus a leather and skins corner. Suddenly you're contemplating not just buttons for your cardi but an entire outfit and coordinating handbag to complete your look.

When you've made your selection(s), take the entire box of buttons to a Mood associate. If you're buying fabric or fringe, take the bolt to a cutting table. Your associate will bag and tag (or measure and cut) your finds. Once you've acquired all your goodies, head to the cash registers near the front entrance. They'll add up all your treasures, just like on *Project Runway*.

On your way out, give Swatch, the resident Boston Terrier, a pat. Then channel Tim Gunn and say "Thank you, Mood!" when you head to the elevator.

Sil Thread Inc.

257 W 38th Street, Manhattan
(212) 997-8949
threadus.com

Need a zipper? In a nonstandard length? And a special color? Sil Thread is the place for you. They stock a wide variety of YKK zippers in various colors with hundreds of tape color options to choose from. When you first look at the zippers, you will think they are all way too long, but the beauty is that Sil will cut any zipper to your specified length and finish off the top properly. No more making do with something that isn't just right. In addition to all those zippers, Sil has, of course, thread in all shades. They also stock Clover (yes, that Clover) accessories, and notions for all kinds of sewing (shoulder pads, bra cups, dress forms, care labels). You will be amazed at how many things you want/need in a place that doesn't sell yarn.

Pacific Trimming + Riri Zipper

218 W 38th Street, Manhattan
(212) 279-9310
pacifictrimming.com

This place is two (or three) shops in one: zippers, buttons, notions. When you walk in you will find rows of chains and ribbon and trimmings sold by the yard. Head to the right for a wide selection of zippers, some precut and others by the foot, in all the varieties you can imagine (metal teeth, plastic teeth, different pulls, tapes, and stoppers—customize away!). To the far right is a room with beads, pompoms, and buttons on cards (also where I buy tiny crochet hooks for beaded knitting). At the back you will find another wide variety of buttons, this time sold from tiny drawers. Very old-school, with a focus on wholesale customers, yet they are friendly and welcoming to everyone.

M+J Trimming

1008 6th Avenue, Manhattan
(800) 965-8746
mjtrim.com

All on one floor, M&J is the place to go for buttons, ribbons, fabric flowers, and everything sparkly. The staff is very knowledgeable, also dressed in black like our friends at Mood, and happy to help you reach down any button box from one of the higher shelves. With a recent reorganization of their space, M&J has created a button room at the back of the store stocking buttons in different shapes, sizes, and materials. Outside of the button room is a massive selection of rhinestones from Swarovski and others, both iron-on and sewable varieties in every color and shape you

can imagine, as well as fabric flowers, patches, and zippers. You will also find walls of ribbon spools, beads, sequins, and edgings from feathers to fringe.

The button storage boxes are set up the same way as at Mood, and their inventory system is similar, so you'll take your choices to an associate for bagging and tagging. Button selection ranges from the gold blazer type with various crests to glass, leather, and horn, all the way to cutesy shapes perfect for that baby sweater you need to finish. Feel free to set up your decision zone on one of the tables they have installed and expect that you may get some useful input from M&J associates and fellow customers. There are, again, discontinued and standard stock items, and M&J does wholesale for large orders.

M&J is wonderfully (dangerously) stocked with craft supplies. Once you find the perfect button to finish off your cardigan, you'll want to create your own feather-trimmed fascinators and add pins and patches to all your clothes. They even have notions like purse handles and fur pompoms. Every time I visit, I come away with a stack of new ideas and a lighter wallet.

There may not be any notions here, but there is one more can't-miss spot in the Garment District for any knitter...

Kinokuniya

1073 6th Avenue, Manhattan
(212) 869-1700
usa.kinokuniya.com

A Japanese bookstore across from Bryant Park? What could such a place have to do with knitters? Well, walk in, avoid the well-stocked shelves of literature and art and head down the stairs. Promise yourself to check out the pens, notebooks, and other delights near the bottom of the stairs, then head for the craft book section, where you will find a collection of wonderful knitting books, both charming pattern collections and spellbinding stitch dictionaries. Since most Japanese patterns are presented in chart form, once you decipher the basics of the chart, you open up a whole new world of knitting (and crochet—Japanese books do not differentiate between the two,

so don't be surprised to find crochet sections in what would seem, at first glance, to be a knitting book). If those books aren't enough, be sure to check out the sewing and style books in the vicinity, the fashion books on the main floor, and the large collection of manga upstairs. After making your choices (it's so hard to decide!) and paying at the first floor checkout, head upstairs to the café to grab some sushi or Japanese pastries to cap off your visit.

Another not-to-miss bookstore south of Union Square...

The Strand

828 Broadway, Manhattan
(212) 473-1452
strandbooks.com

Their motto is "18 Miles of Books," and they are not kidding around. The Strand stocks new, used, and rare books over multiple floors. Happily, they have a robust Knitting section up on the second floor, as well as a great Fashion section. They also have *every other book you can imagine*, plus great souvenirs, like their own branded totes, mugs, t-shirts, Moleskine notebooks (my fave), and much more. The Strand also hosts author readings and signings, including Clara Parkes, so be sure to check their event calendar. When you see the red awnings and used-book carts, you've found it!

And one special spot away from the Garment District...

Tender Buttons

143 E 62nd Street, Manhattan
(212) 758-7004
tenderbuttons-nyc.com

Do not miss this Upper East Side treasure box. From the building it's housed in, to the giant gold button marking the entrance, to the checkerboard floor and hand-lettered labels on the button boxes, this place is old-world and filled with charm. When you are looking for a button that is special, antique, or one-of-a-kind, Tender Buttons is the place to go. Eighteenth-century Wedgwood, reverse-painted glass and copper, Liberty silver, and many more rare buttons are featured alongside Bakelite, horn, metal, and mother-of-pearl. The long narrow space has boxes of buttons floor-to-ceiling on one side, glass display cases for the rare and precious along the other wall, and little drop-leaf tables with Thonet chairs down the middle, so you can sit and make the perfect choice for your project. Like other button shops, each box contains a variety of buttons, but Tender Buttons handwrites each description, so the entire presentation feels extra-special. For payment, be sure to bring cash. Luckily there are banks with ATMs just around the corner. This tiny shop is sure to have the perfect finish for you project (or the starting point for a new one—sometimes a sweater begins with a button).

Manhattanhenge

Kathleen Dames

Just as the sun aligns itself directly along the Manhattan street grid twice a year (the phenomenon known as "Manhattanhenge," when the island's rakish 29-degree angle lines up with the ever-shifting rise/set point of the sun), these gloves have fingers in alternating colors. You see the sun peeking through the buildings, right? The most dramatic viewing takes place in Midtown thanks to the skyscraper canyons, but you can experience the magical alignment anywhere on the island by facing east at sunrise or west at sunset.

The gloves, worked from the fingertips down, are finished off with chevron cuffs to match the cozy cowl. Various i-cord techniques, including i-cord fingers, will see you through this project. The Manhattanhenge Chevron slip stitch pattern will have you playing with color even if you have always stuck to one shade. You'll be ready for the next 'henge in no time.

Sizes
Cowl: One Size
Gloves: S (M, L) shown in size M

Finished Measurements
Cowl: 9 inches/23 cm deep, 25 inches/63.5 cm circumference
Gloves: 6 (6 ½, 7) inches/15 (16.5, 18) cm hand circumference

Materials
Backyard Fiberworks Meadow Light (80% merino, 10% cashmere, 10% nylon; 435 yds/398 m per 3.5 oz/100 g skein)
   Color A: Stormcloud; 1 skein for all sizes
   Color B: Urchin; 1 skein for all sizes
US0/1.75 mm set of DPNs (or size needed to achieve gauge)
US3/3.25 mm 24-inch/60-cm circular needle (or size needed to achieve gauge)
B/1 crochet hook (or size close to smaller needle)
Coil-less safety pins or locking stitch markers (two), stitch marker, waste yarn, tapestry needle

Gauge
32 sts x 40 rows = 4 inches/10 cm in Stockinette Stitch with smaller needles for gloves, after blocking
24 sts x 24 rows = 3 inches/7.5 cm in Zebra Chevron Stitch with larger needles for cuffs and cowl, after blocking

NOTES

- The dirty little secret about gloves is that if you can get the fiddly finger and thumb bits out of the way first, they are fun and quick to knit. So, why not start at the top? And the weird thing about gloves is that all the fingers on your hand have more or less the same circumference (I have scrawny pinkies, but I'm willing to overlook it). Plus, the pointer and ring fingers are pretty much the same length, as are the thumb and pinky. Finger lengths given are for standard measurements, so be sure to measure your own fingers for a custom fit.

- Of course, fingers may be knit all in one color, but I worked the pointer and ring fingers in Color B to enhance the "sunrise aligned with the Manhattan grid" effect that inspired the gloves in the first place.

- If you have ever made an i-cord of more than three stitches, you may have noticed that a ladder forms across the back of the cord. With these gloves you take advantage of that feature by quickly working i-cord to your desired length, then laddering up two new stitches from those rungs formed across the back of the cord. Once blocked you won't be able to tell where those ladders were in the first place.

- Slipped stitch knitting is different than stranded because you only work one color per round. Once you find your rhythm in this intuitive stitch pattern, you will finish quickly, and you will have a cozy, squishy, double-thick fabric to enjoy.

Manhattanhenge Chevron

	V			V			V			V		V				V			V			V			12
	V			V			V			V		V				V			V			V			11
V			V			V			V				V			V			V			V		10
V			V			V			V				V			V			V			V		9
	V			V			V			V		V				V			V			V	8
	V			V			V			V		V				V			V			V	7
V			V			V			V		V				V			V			V		6
V			V			V			V		V				V			V			V		5
V			V			V			V				V			V			V			V		4
V			V			V			V				V			V			V			V		3
	V			V			V			V		V				V			V			V	2
	V			V			V			V		V				V			V			V	1

24 23 22 21 20 19 18 17 16 15 14 13 12 11 10 9 8 7 6 5 4 3 2 1

Chart Key
▢ = Color A
▢ = Color B
▢ = knit
[V] = sl wyib
▢ = repeat

Manhattanhenge Chevron Instructions

Rnds 1 & 2: With Color B (Sl1, k2) nine times.

Rnds 3 & 4: With Color A k1, (sl1, k2) four times, k1, (sl1, k2) three times, sl1.

Rnds 5 & 6: With Color B (k2, sl1) four times, k1, (sl1, k2) three times, sl1, k1.

Rnds 7 & 8: With Color A (Sl1, k2) nine times.

Rnds 9 & 10: With Color B k1, (sl1, k2) four times, k1, (sl1, k2) three times, sl1.

Rnds 11 & 12: With Color B (k2, sl1) four times, k1, (sl1, k2) three times, sl1, k1.

PATTERN

Cowl

With larger ndls and Color A, provisionally CO 192 sts. Join for working in the rnd, being careful not to twist and pl m to indicate BOR. With Colors A & B, work Manhattanhenge Chevron eight times around until piece measures 9 inches/23 cm. Break Color B. With Color A, work I-cord BO (see Techniques, p. 67). Undo provisional CO and repeat I-cord BO with Color A for second edge.

Gloves (make two)

Pinky/thumb (make two)
With DPN and Color A, CO 6 (7, 8) sts. Slide sts along DPN from left end of ndl to right to work a new row, gently stretch working yarn across back of sts. Knit one row. Increase row: *K1, m1; repeat from * 6 (7, 8) times total—12 (14, 16) sts. Work i-cord until piece measures 1 ¾ (2, 2 ¼) inches from CO edge. Break yarn, with crochet hook ladder up two sts from CO edge to live sts, and set aside on spare ndl or waste yarn—14 (16, 18) sts.

Ring/index (make two)
With DPN and Color B, CO 6 (7, 8) sts. Slide sts along DPN from left end of ndl to right to work a new row, gently stretch working yarn across back of sts. Knit one row. Increase row: *K1, m1; repeat from * 6 (7, 8) times total—12 (14, 16) sts. Work i-cord until piece measures 2 ¼ (2 ½, 2 ¾) inches from CO edge. Break yarn, with crochet hook ladder up two sts from CO edge to live sts, and set aside on spare ndl or waste yarn—14 (16, 18) sts.

Middle finger (make one)
With DPN and Color A, CO 6 (7, 8) sts. Slide sts along DPN from left end of ndl to right to work a new row, gently stretch working yarn across back of sts. Knit one row. Increase row: *K1, m1; repeat from * 6 (7, 8) times total—12 (14, 16) sts. Work i-cord until piece measures 2 ½ (2 ¾, 3) inches from CO edge. Break yarn, with crochet hook ladder up two sts from CO edge to live sts, and set aside on spare ndl or waste yarn—14 (16, 18) sts.

Hand
Join pointer, middle, and ring fingers together as follows: Sl7 (8, 9) sts of pointer onto DPN leaving remaining sts on waste yarn, slip 7 (8, 9) sts of middle finger onto DPN leaving remaining sts on waste yarn, sl7 (8, 9) sts of ring finger onto DPN, then onto second DPN sl7 (8, 9) ring finger sts, 7 (8, 9) middle finger sts, and 7 (8, 9) pointer finger sts—42 (48, 54) sts. With COlor A k6 (7, 8), k2tog (last st of pointer with first st of middle), k5 (6, 7), k2tog, k12 (14, 16), k2tog, k5 (6, 7), k2tog, k6 (7, 8)—38 (44, 50) sts.
Stitch crossing rnd 1: K6 (7, 8), sl1 to coil-less pin and hold to back of work, k5 (6, 7), sl1 to coil-less pin and hold to back of work, k12 (14, 16), sl pinned st to left ndl and k1, sl1 to coil-less pin and hold to back of work, k6 (7, 8), slip pinned st to left ndl and k1, sl1 to coil-less pin and hold to back of work, k6 (7, 8).
Stitch crossing rnd 2: K6 (7, 8), slip pinned st to left ndl and k1, k5 (6, 7), sl pinned st to left ndl and k1, knit to end.
Join pinky: Sl6 (7, 8) pinky sts to spare DPN, then sl remaining 6 (7, 8) pinky sts to second DPN; k18 (21, 24) sts of hand, k2tog (last st of hand with first st of pinky), k5 (6, 7); k5 (6, 7) pinky sts from second DPN, k2tog (last st of pinky with first of hand), k18 (21, 24) sts—48 (56, 64) sts.
Stitch crossing rnd 3: K18 (21, 24) sts, sl1 to coil-less pin and hold to back of work, k10 (12, 14), sl pinned st to left ndl and k1, sl1 to coil-less pin and hold to back of work, k18 (21, 24) sts.
Stitch crossing rnd 4: K29 (34, 39) sts, sl pinned st to left ndl and k1, knit to end.
Work even until hand measures ¾ (1, 1 ¼) inches from the base of the pointer finger. On last rnd, stop 1 st before end.
Join thumb: Sl7 (8, 9) thumb sts to spare DPN, then slip remaining thumb sts to second DPN; k2tog (last st of hand with

first st of thumb), k6 (7, 8) sts, pl m to indicate BOR, k6 (7, 8) sts, k2tog (last st of thumb with first st of hand), k46 (54, 62) sts, sl1 to coil-less pin and hold to back of work, knit to end.
Stitch crossing rnd 5: K6 (7, 8) sts, sl pinned st to left ndl and k1, sl1 to pin and hold to back of work, pl m for thumb gusset, k46 (54, 62) sts, pl m for thumb gusset, slip pinned st to left ndl and k1, knit to end.
Thumb decrease rnd: Knit to 2 sts before m, k2tog, sl m, knit to next m, sl m, ssk, knit to end—2 sts dec'd.
Work two rnds even.
Repeat these three rows until 2 sts remain between markers.
Final thumb decrease rnd: Sl1, remove m, sl1 back to left ndl, k2tog, knit to 1 st before m, sl1 k-wise, remove m, ssk with just-slipped st and st after m—48 (56, 64) sts. Work even ½ inch or desired length to top of wrist.
On last rnd for size S, work even—48 sts.
On last rnd for size M, (k14, m1) four times—60 sts.
On last rnd for size L, (k14, k2tog) four times—60 sts.

Cuff
Switch to larger ndl and knit 1 rnd. Work Manhattanhenge Chevron over 48 (60, 60) sts (sts 1–24 twice, then for larger sizes sts 1–12 once more). Continue working chart until cuff measures 3 inches. Break Color B, then CO 3 sts with Color A onto left ndl. Work I-cord BO across all sts. Break yarn and use tail to attach end of i-cord to beginning.

FINISHING
Weave in all ends. Block to finished measurements.

Metropolitan Opera

Lars Rains

Whenever I would go to see a production at the Metropolitan Opera, I was always awestruck by how the chandeliers silently ascend towards the ceiling as a cue to the audience that the opera was about to start. Such drama, even before a single note is sung!

For this Fair Isle hat, I wanted to recreate the impression of these bright lights against a dark background of shadows. By the way, it is perfectly normal to hear the overture of your favorite opera start in your head as you knit this hat.

Sizes
Adult S/M (L/XL) shown in size S/M

Finished Measurements
Circumference: 19 ¾ (24 ¾) inches/50 (63) cm
Height: 9½ (10½) inches/24 (26.5) cm

Materials
Backyard Fiberworks Meadow Light Metropolitan Opera Kit (80% merino, 10% cashmere, 10% nylon; 133 yds/122 m
   per 1.2 oz/33 g skein); 1 kit
     Color A: Deep Creek; 2 mini skeins for all sizes
     Color B: Natural; 1 mini skein for all sizes
     Color C: Marigold; 1 mini skein for all sizes
US3/3.25mm 16-inch/40-cm circular needle (or one size smaller than gauge needle)
US4/3.5mm 16-inch/40-cm circular needle + set of DPNs (or size needed to achieve gauge)
Stitch marker, tapestry needle

Gauge
29 sts x 32 rounds = 4 inches/10 cm in Stockinette Stitch with larger needle, after blocking

PATTERN

Brim

With smaller circular ndl and Color A, CO 144 (180) sts. Join for working in the rnd, being careful not to twist. Pl m to indicate BOR.

Rnd 1: (K2, p2) around.

Repeat Rnd 1 eleven more times.

Body

Switch to larger ndl and knit 6 rnds.

With Color A, Color B, and Color C, work Rnds 1–27 of Metropolitan Opera chart. Break Colors B & C.

With Color A, knit 6 rnds.

Crown

Note: Switch to preferred method for small-circumference knitting when needed.

Size L/XL Only: (K13, ssk) around—168 sts. Knit 2 rnds. (K12, k2tog) around—156 sts. Knit 2 rnds. (K11, ssk) around—144 sts. Knit 2 rnds.

All sizes: (K10, k2tog) around—132 sts. Knit 2 rnds. (K9, ssk) around—120 sts. Knit 2 rnds. (K8, k2tog) around—108 sts. Knit 2 rnds. (K7, ssk) around—96 sts. Knit 2 rnds. (K6, k2tog) around—84 sts. Knit 2 rnds. (K5, ssk) around—72 sts. Knit 2 rnds. (K4, k2tog) around—60 sts. Knit 2 rnds. (K3, ssk) around—48 sts. Knit 2 rnds. (K2, k2tog) around—36 sts. Knit 2 rnds. (K1, ssk) around—24 sts. Knit 2 rnds. (K2tog) around—12 sts. Break working yarn and pull through remaining 12 sts.

FINISHING

Weave in all ends with tapestry needle. Block to finished measurements.

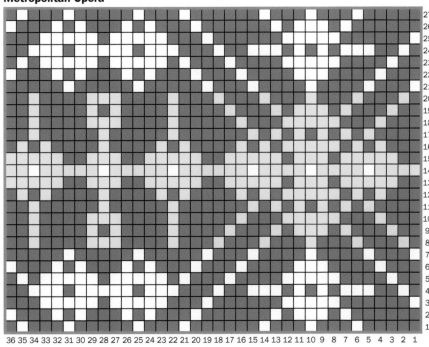

Metropolitan Opera

27
26
25
24
23
22
21
20
19
18
17
16
15
14
13
12
11
10
9
8
7
6
5
4
3
2
1

36 35 34 33 32 31 30 29 28 27 26 25 24 23 22 21 20 19 18 17 16 15 14 13 12 11 10 9 8 7 6 5 4 3 2 1

Chart Key

☐ = knit with color indicated

☐ = repeat

Color Legend

■ = Color A: Deep Creek

☐ = Color B: Natural

▨ = Color C: Marigold

Kathleen Loves NY

Books

97 Orchard: An Edible History of Five Immigrant Families in One New York Tenement by Jane Ziegelman—Read, visit the Tenement Museum on the Lower East Side, then eat at Katz's.

The Cricket in Times Square by George Selden and Garth Williams—A magical book about a humble cricket.

Eloise by Kay Thompson—Don't you want to live at the Plaza?

From the Mixed-Up Files of Mrs. Basil E. Frankweiler by E.L. Konigsburg—And now you want to live at the Met!

The Great Gatsby by F. Scott Fitzgerald—A classic for a reason.

Harriet the Spy by Louise Fitzhugh—Now you want an egg cream.

The Island at the Center of the World by Russell Shorto—Manhattan's fascinating early history as a Dutch colony.

Kitchen Confidential by Anthony Bourdain—No fish on Tuesdays.

Stuart Little by E.B. White—Another little character with a big heart (plus sailing model boats in Central Park).

Through the Children's Gate by Adam Gopnik—The adventure of raising a family in New York City.

Movies

All About Eve—"It's going to be a bumpy night."

Bill Cunningham New York—Bill's devotion to personal style.

Desperately Seeking Susan—When the East Village was gritty.

Elf—Holidays are the best in the Big Apple, plus Peter Dinklage.

The Fifth Element—Taxis are the same no matter the century.

Ghostbusters—The reboot for Kate McKinnon and Leslie Jones; the original for Bill Murray and their firehouse HQ.

Metropolitan—Upper class New Yorkers during "deb" season.

Rear Window—So much happens in such a tiny apartment.

When Harry Met Sally—Katz's, the Met, Carrie Fisher!

Working Girl—Staten Island girl takes Manhattan in the '80s.

TV shows

30 Rock—Tina Fey is my spirit animal.

Broad City—High hilarity in Abbi & Ilana's NYC.

The Dick Van Dyke Show—Where Mary Tyler Moore got her start.

Fame—"I'm gonna live forever!"

Gossip Girl—Teenage New York soap opera. So addictive.

Master of None—Great, modern multicultural comedy.

The Real Housewives of New York City—My guilty pleasure. So many women behaving badly, right in my own city.

Saturday Night Live—Over forty years and still going strong.

Ugly Betty—Fashion publishing in the early aughts. So fun.

Unbreakable Kimmy Schmidt—Hilarious, absurd, filmed nearby.

Eateries/drinkeries

Bonchon Chicken—Tasty Korean fried chicken in the Garment District (and other locations). Don't miss the seasoned fries and starters. Perfect for lunch when you're on a #buttonhunt.

Grom—Cap off your pizza at John's (just down the street, plus two additional locations around town) with gelato made "like it used to be." Apparently, there are other flavors, but it's only Nocciola (hazelnut) for me.

Ippudo NY—Grab a lunch of delicious ramen after visiting The Strand (or check out the West Side location). The space is very cool, and communal tables mean you can check out what everyone else is slurping.

John's Pizzeria on Bleeker Street—Delicious coal-fired brick-oven pizza (their sausage is amazing), since 1929. As Zagat's says, "worth the wait in line"—go early, then it's no problem. Cash only, but they have an ATM near the loo.

Mariebelle—The best hot chocolate is in the most charming space (conveniently near Purl Soho). They sell fancy chocolates too, but the little cafe in the back is the secret treasure.

Mermaid Inn—At multiple locations around the city you can get your fix of lobster rolls, Old Bay fries, and tasty beverages in charming B&W spaces. Friendly staff plus complimentary chocolate pudding for dessert.

Old Town Bar—One of the quintessential Old New York watering holes with a marble and mahogany bar, tin ceiling, and a dumbwaiter. Not far from The Strand.

The Oyster Bar at Grand Central—Counter service is so fun, as is the saloon. I'm partial to the scallop pan roast with a gimlet, but start with some raw oysters. Be sure to have some $1s for the attendant in the ladies room (so old school).

Souvlaki GR—Delicious Greek food from the tzatziki and homemade pita to the souvlaki (I like it with shrimp). Decorated like a charming blue and white taverna, if you're lucky you'll get the "upstairs" booth at the Stanton Street location (there's one near Carnegie Hall, too). The Oia Sunset is my birthday drink.

Veselka—What seems like a 24-hour diner is one of the last bastions of the East Village Ukrainian neighborhood. Get the meat plate (comes with beet horseradish sauce—so good), and if you're lucky, they'll have Christmas Borscht on the menu. You can walk over to Downtown Yarns from here.

Opal
Clock

Kathleen Dames

Did you know that the crown jewel of Grand Central Terminal sits atop the information booth in the Main Hall and is literally a jewel? The Opal Clock, with its four helpful faces made of opal, is valued at over $10 million USD.

Just as the clock is perfectly aligned with the Terminal's axis, the center-start of this stole sets up four circular cables emerging from a braided base. Edges are finished with two kinds of i-cord, while each end is filled with smaller versions of the clock cable. Opal Clock works up quickly in Backyard Fiberworks's luscious Homestead to keep you cozy, but the novel construction and clever cables will make you wish for more.

Sizes
One Size

Finished Measurements
Width: 16 inches/41 cm
Length: 60 inches/152.5 cm

Materials
Backyard Fiberworks Homestead (80% merino, 10% cashmere, 10% nylon; 181 yds/165 m per 3.5 oz/100 g skein);
    color: Silver Spring; 4 skeins
US7/4.5 mm set of DPNs and 40-inch/100-cm circular needle (or size needed to achieve gauge)
Stitch markers, tapestry needle

Gauge
18 sts x 24 rows = 4 inches/10cm in Stockinette Stitch, after blocking

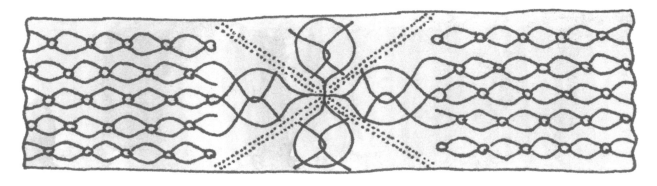

Opal Clock Center Motif

NOTES

- Along the sides of the central panel, the Single or Double I-cord Bindoff finishes one or two stitches at a time to prevent the edge from flaring (see Techniques, p. 67). More stitches are required for the cable than would be needed for a simple stockinette fabric, so we eliminate those in a tidy way.
- Working two additional rows of i-cord unattached at each corner eases the cord around the edge of the wrap.

PATTERN

Center Panel

With DPN CO 8 sts. Distribute sts evenly over four ndls and work with fifth. Join sts for working in the rnd, being careful not to twist.
Rnd 1: *K1, yo, kfbf, yo; repeat from * three more times—24 sts.
Rnd 2: Knit all sts.
Rnd 3: *K1, yo, kfb five times, yo; repeat from * three more times—52 sts.
Begin working Opal Clock Center Motif Rnd 4 and continue through Rnd 58. Corner sts are not charted and should be knit on all rnds. Switch to circular ndl when sts no longer comfortably fit on DPNs.

Side 1 (first edge of square)

Turn work and with WS facing CO 3 sts onto left ndl. Work Single I-cord BO 15 times (see Techniques), then work Double I-cord BO twice. Work Single I-cord BO 8 times, work Double I-cord BO 6 times, work Single I-cord BO 8 times, work Double I-cord BO twice, work Single I-cord BO 15 times. On last Single I-cord BO leave the 3 sts on the right ndl.

Side 2 Panel

Side 2 setup row (WS): K2, m1-k, k1, p5, m1-p, p2, k4, m1-p, p1, k2, p2, k1, m1-k, k2, p2, k2, m1-p, p1, k4, p1, m1-p, p5, m1-p, k4, p1, m1-p, k2, p2, k1, m1-k, k2, p2, k2, m1-p, p1, k4, p1, m1-p, p6, m1-k, k3—83 sts.
Sts for Sides 3 & 4 remain on ndl to be worked in turn.
Turn work and CO 3 sts onto left ndl. Work 3 sts Side I-cord (see Techniques, p. 67), then work Row 2 of Opal Clock Side Panel over 80 sts (sts 1–32 twice followed by sts 1–16 sts again) to last 3 sts, wyif sl3 p-wise—86 sts.
Continue working Opal Clock Side Panel and following Side I-cord instructions ending on Row 17 of fifth repeat.

Finish Side 2
At beginning of next RS Row work Side I-cord Row 4 twice, then, finish the side panel by working Single I-cord BO 20 times, Double I-cord BO 4 times, Single I-cord BO 24 times, Double I-cord BO 4 times, Single I-cord BO 20 times, then 2 rows of unattached I-cord. Break yarn and weave together side and end I-cord sts.

Side 3 (across square from Side 1)

With WS facing rejoin yarn at right edge of Side 3, then repeat Side 1.

Side 4 Panel

Repeat Side 2 Panel on Side 4. At beginning of second row, pick up 3 sts from base of I-cord for right I-cord edging, then continue following Side 2 Panel.

FINISHING

Weave in all ends. Block to finished measurements.

Opal Clock Center Motif

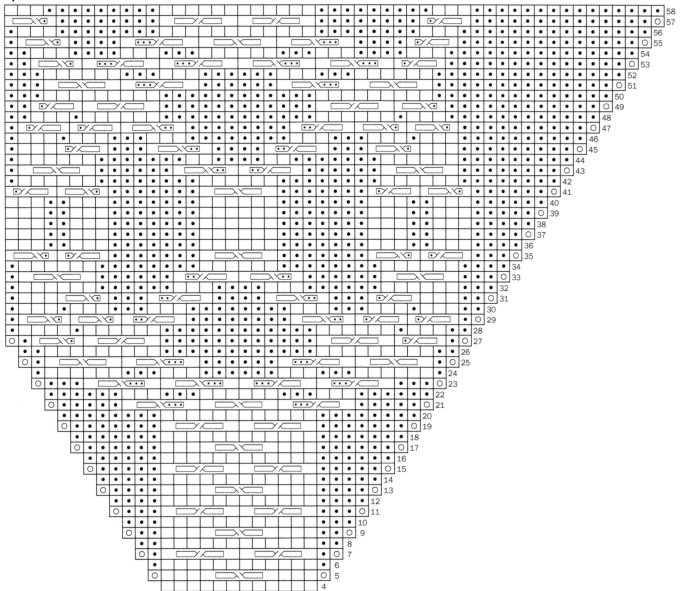

Chart Key

☐ = knit

● = purl

⬜▷◁⬜ = sl2 to cn to back, k2, k2 from cn

⬜▷◁⬜ = sl2 to cn to back, k2, p2 from cn

⬜◁▷⬜ = sl2 to cn to front, k2, k2 from cn

⬜◁▷⬜ = sl2 to cn to front, p2, k2 from cn

⬜▷◁⬜ = sl1 to cn to back, k3, p1 from cn

⬜◁▷⬜ = sl3 to cn to front, p1, k3 from cn

⬜▷◁⬜ = sl2 to cn to back, k3, p2 from cn

⬜◁▷⬜ = sl3 to cn to front, p2, k3 from cn

⬜▷◁⬜ = sl3 to cn to back, k3, k3 from cn

⬜▷◁⬜ = sl3 to cn to back, k3, p3 from cn

⬜◁▷⬜ = sl3 to cn to front, k3, k3 from cn

⬜◁▷⬜ = sl3 to cn to front, p3, k3 from cn

☐ = repeat

Opal Clock Side Panel

47

NYC Yarn Crawl

Lisa Chamoff

You know you can find anything (everything!) in New York City, from designer clothing to vintage threads, from obscure ingredients to handcrafted jewelry. Home to several local yarn stores, each of which sparkles with its own special vibe and niche products, plus classes and events that foster community amongst local crafters. Plan your visit for mid-September, and you can be part of the annual NYC Yarn Crawl. Whenever you come to town, be sure to visit these shops.

NYC Local Yarn Shops

1. **Annie & Company**
2. **Argyle Yarn Shop**
3. **Brooklyn General Store**
4. **Downtown Yarns**
5. **Knitty City**
6. **Purl Soho**
7. **String Thing Studio**
8. **String Yarns**
9. **Woolyn**

Brooklyn
2, 3, 7, 9

Annie + Company

1763 Second Avenue, Manhattan
(212) 289-2944
annieandco.com

Part LYS and part needlepoint store, Annie Goodman's eponymous shop on Manhattan's Upper East Side caters to crafters of both varieties equally. On the knitting side, Annie's stocks reasonably-priced basics from brands such as Classic Elite and Sirdar, more luxurious lines from small overseas companies like The Fibre Company and Manos del Uruguay, and it receives regular shipments of Madelinetosh. The shop often hosts special trunk shows by both local and national indie dyers.

Argyle Yarn Shop

288 Prospect Park West, Brooklyn
(347) 227-7799

argyleyarnshop.com

Located in the heart of Prospect Park-adjacent Windsor Terrace, this welcoming shop is a true "mom and pop" operation. Husband-and-wife owners David and Esther Betten fill their store with a wide range of yarns, from mainstream brands including Bernat, Berroco, and Cascade, to hand dyes from Ireland's Hedgehog Fibres, London's Qing Fibre, and New Hampshire's Woolen Boon. It also boasts one of the most extensive collections of American wool yarn from Maine-based Quince & Co.

Brooklyn General Store

128 Union Street, Brooklyn
(718) 237-7753

brooklyngeneral.com

Housed in a former department store on the outskirts of the quaint Carroll Gardens neighborhood, Brooklyn General has the charm of an old-fashioned haberdashery and is a destination for the multicraftual knitter. Rustic and luxurious yarns—from dyers and small companies including Hudson Valley-based Jill Draper Makes Stuff, Canada's Northbound Knitting, and Brooklyn Tweed—fill the walls of shelves outfitted with original rolling ladders. Owner Catherine Clark, who also runs a midwifery practice across the street, sells a wide variety of fabric and sewing patterns, offering classes in not only knitting, sewing, and quilting, but also felting, spinning, rug hooking, and embroidery.

Downtown Yarns

45 Avenue A, Manhattan
(212) 995-5991

downtownyarns.com

Step through the screen door into this small, homey shop in Manhattan's formerly edgy East Village. Its rustic wood shelves house a well-curated selection of staple yarns, including Brown Sheep, Debbie Bliss, and Plymouth, along with a variety of self-striping Noro and hand-dyed skeins from Madelinetosh, Malabrigo, and The Yarns of Rhichard Devrieze. Opened in 2001 by former florist Rita Bobry, it's one of the city's oldest LYSes. Don't forget to give shop dog Zach a few head scratches.

Knitty City

208 West 79th Street, Manhattan
(212) 787-5896

knittycitynyc.com

This welcoming shop on Manhattan's bustling Upper West Side bursts with colorful mountains of stock containing a variety of treasures, including hand-dyed yarn from Freia, Julie Asselin, and SweetGeorgia, local indies like Nooch Fiber, and quirky knitting-related gifts. The appropriately named owner, Pearl Chin, also has one of the city's most comprehensive collections of knitting, crochet, and needle art books, magazines, and patterns, and regularly hosts book signings and special events, as well as community events like the Pussy Hat Project, Welcome Blanket Knitalong, Knitted Knockers meetups, Men's Knit Night, and a monthly book club.

Purl Soho

459 Broome Street, Manhattan
(212) 420-8796
purlsoho.com

Now a well-known brand with a popular line of free patterns, Purl started as two tiny shops on Sullivan Street, merging in 2010 to create the crafting megaboutique, surrounded by high-end clothing stores on Broome Street in Soho (a.k.a. South of Houston). They stock Purl's house line of merino, cashmere, alpaca, cotton, silk, and linen yarns, as well as a nice assortment of Anzula, Madelinetosh, and mYak, a New York City company that sources its yak fiber from a Tibetan cooperative. They also stock fabric by the yard and bundle, and kits for a variety of crafts, including embroidery and jewelry making.

String Yarns

144 East 74th Street, 2nd Floor, Manhattan
(212) 288-9276
stringyarns.com

Perched above Lexington Avenue, this shop on Manhattan's tony Upper East Side is known for its exclusive designs and services that include customized patterns and professional finishing. Fiber industry veteran Stacy Charles purchased the business from founder Linda Morse in 2015 and the shop carries plenty of Stacy Charles yarn, along with balls and hanks from New York-based Artyarns, Italy's Filatura Di Crosa, and June Cashmere from Kyrgyzstan, as well its own line of custom-milled yarn. String also hosts unique workshops from well-known designers.

String Thing Studio

54 7th Avenue, Brooklyn
(929) 337-6130
stringthingstudio.com

Longtime knitter Felicia Eve has opened one of New York's newest yarn shops. The cozy space features a large, peaceful back garden that serves as a community gathering place, hosting everything from family-friendly parties to dyeing classes. The selection here includes a mix of reasonably priced staples and unique yarns, including Clinton Hill Cashmere, a bespoke yarn line named for the owner's Brooklyn neighborhood and milled in Italy, and our favorite—Backyard Fiberworks.

Woolyn

105 Atlantic Avenue, Brooklyn
(718) 522-5820
woolyn.com

This bright shop, tucked amidst the high-end boutiques and Middle Eastern food stores on busy Atlantic Avenue, specializes in all things indie and local. The majority of its cubbies are filled with hand-dyed yarn, including some from NYC indie dyers like Yarn Over New York and Asylum Fibers, and owner Rachel Maurer also stocks project bags and stitch markers from Brooklyn makers. The shop also has one of the most extensive collections of spinning fiber in the city, along with Ashford and Schacht spinning wheels and classes that include beginner spinning and weaving.

Lisa Loves NY

Tell us a New York story (brush with fame, hidden treasure, New York-iest adventure):

I actually have a knitting-related one: One Sunday afternoon when I was knitting in Madison Square Park, I was approached by Brandon Stanton, the guy behind *Humans of New York*. He photographed me knitting and asked me questions, including one about my greatest knitting triumph, which I told him was frogging and reknitting almost an entire sweater. It was published in October 2014, a week before my first Rhinebeck Trunk Show!

Subway knitting: must-have or never ever?

Must have. You never know when you're going to be stuck underground for an hour (or more).

Favorite station?

The Smith/9th Street F stop in Brooklyn has one of the most beautiful views of the NYC skyline.

Favorite neighborhood?

Mine!—Ditmas Park. I love the diversity and community spirit; the main drag, Cortelyou Road, is lined with small businesses, including great restaurants, bars and the Brooklyn Artery, which sells locally-made greeting cards, food, jewelry and other gifts. All that's missing is a yarn store…

Mets or Yankees?

Mets—I grew up on Long Island and one of my earliest memories is of the Mets winning the 1986 World Series.

Picker or thrower?

Thrower.

Project monogamy or cast on all the things?

I'm generally monogamous, but do have several WIPs at one time for different settings (like knit night knitting, TV knitting, etc.).

Favorite places to eat/drink/knit in NYC?

Very hard to choose, but among my favorites: In my old neighborhood, the Waterfront Ale House for great beer and food (fun fact: it's not actually by the water!) and Riverpark for special occasions; Molyvos for a post-theater dinner, Frankies Spuntino in Carroll Gardens, Bennie Thai Cafe in the Financial District. I love knitting in the back gardens at Qathra (a coffee shop), Bar Chord, and Hinterlands Bar in my current neighborhood.

Movies

1. *Working Girl*
2. *When Harry Met Sally*
3. *West Side Story*
4. *Big*
5. *The Muppets Take Manhattan*
6. *Coming To America*
7. *Three Men and a Baby*
8. *Annie* (the 1982 version)
9. *The Warriors*
10. *You've Got Mail*

TV Shows

1. *Mad Men*
2. *Sex and the City*
3. *Seinfeld*
4. *Friends*
5. *All in the Family*
6. *Diff'rent Strokes*
7. *Night Court*
8. *How I Met Your Mother*
9. *The Patty Duke Show*
10. *Taxi*

Songs

1. "Bleecker Street" by Simon & Garfunkel
2. "I and Love and You" by The Avett Brothers
3. "I'm Waiting for the Man" by The Velvet Underground
4. "Ditmas" by Mumford & Sons (named after my neighborhood, where it was recorded!)
5. "Fairytale of New York" by The Pogues
6. "Positively 4th Street" by Bob Dylan
7. "New York State of Mind" by Billy Joel
8. "Tom's Diner" by Suzanne Vega
9. "New York, I Love You But You're Bringing Me Down" by LCD Soundsystem
10. "Out of Habit" by Ani Difranco

Books

1. *Lush Life* by Richard Price
2. *Angels in America* by Tony Kushner (play)
3. *Modern Lovers* by Emma Staub
4. *The Age of Innocence* by Edith Wharton
5. *The Bonfire of the Vanities* by Tom Wolfe
6. *The Heidi Chronicles* by Wendy Wasserstein (play)
7. *Motherless Brooklyn* by Jonathan Lethem
8. *Extremely Loud and Incredibly Close* by Jonathan Safran Foer
9. *The Bell Jar* by Sylvia Plath
10. *The Girls' Guide to Hunting and Fishing* by Melissa Bank

Rockefeller Center

Xandy Peters

This tee is inspired by the majestic art deco architecture of midtown Manhattan. One of the best known examples of this style is Rockefeller Center, a complex of over a dozen skyscrapers, open air shopping areas, multiple works of public art, and the famous ice skating rink, home of the largest Christmas tree in Manhattan.

The neck of the tee has a geometric drop stitch lace openwork motif which can be worn facing front or back. On the opposite side there is a V neck with a single i-cord strap across the deepest part of the V and a curved hem. The sides feature a twisted ribbing detail which continues onto the sleeves. The top is worked from the bottom up in one piece with gentle shaping and articulated raglan sleeves.

Sizes

XS (S, M, L, 1X, 2X, 3X) shown in size S with 1 inch/2.5 cm positive ease

Finished Measurements

Bust: 29 ¼ (33, 37, 40 ¾, 44 ½, 48 ¼, 52 ½) inches/ 74.5 (84, 94, 103.5, 113, 122.5, 133.5) cm

Materials

Backyard Fiberworks Terrain (100% superwash merino; 328 yd/316 m per 3.5 oz/100 g skein); color: Shell; 2 (2, 3, 3, 3, 4, 4) skeins
US4/3.5mm 24-inch/60 cm circular needle + set of DPNs (or one size smaller than gauge needle)
US5/3.75mm 24-inch/60 cm circular needle (or size needed to achieve gauge)
Stitch markers, tapestry needle, steamer (for blocking)

Gauge

25 sts x 32 rows (or rnds, as applicable) = 4 inches/10 cm in Stockinette Stitch with larger needle, after blocking

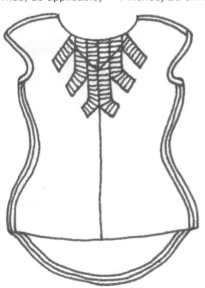

finished bust
29 ¼ (33, 37, 40 ¾, 44 ½, 48 ¼, 52 ½) inches
74.5 (84, 94, 103.5, 113, 122.5, 133.5) cm

front length (from underarm)
20 (20, 21 ½, 22, 22 ¾, 23 ½, 23 ¾) inches
51 (51, 54.5, 56, 58, 59.5, 60.5) cm

back length
22 ¾ (23, 25, 25 ¾, 27, 28 ¼, 29 ½) inches
58 (58.5, 63.5, 65.5, 68.5, 72, 75) cm

lowest point of cutout
9 ½ (10, 10 ½, 11 ¼, 12, 13 ¼, 14) inches
24 (25.5, 26.5, 28.5, 30.5, 33.5, 35.5) cm

neck depth
5 (5 ¼, 5 ¾, 6 ¼, 6 ¾, 7 ¾, 8 ¼) inches
12.5 (13.5, 14.5, 16, 17, 19.5, 21) cm

PATTERN

Setup

With larger ndl, CO 196 (220, 244, 268, 292, 316, 344) sts, pl m, and join for working in the rnd being careful not to twist.

Rnd 1: Purl 1 rnd.

Rnd 2: K10 (12, 14, 16, 18, 20, 24), pl m, k17 (20, 22, 25, 28, 31, 37), pl m, k65 (71, 79, 85, 91, 97, 97), pl m, k18 (21, 23, 26, 29, 32, 38), pl m, k10 (12, 14, 16, 18, 20, 24), pl m, k37 (41, 45, 49, 53, 57, 61), m1-R, k1, m1-L, knit to end of rnd—2 sts inc'd.

Rnd 3: Purl 1 rnd.

Body

Body is worked back and forth with partial (short) rows for the first 38 (42, 46, 50, 54, 58, 62) rows.

Short Row 1: Switch to smaller ndl. Work in Twisted Rib (see Stitches, p. 67) to next m, sl m, m1-R, k to next m, sl m, ssk, k to 2 before next m, k2tog, sl m, k to 1 st before next m, m1-L, p1, sl-m, work in Twisted Rib to next m, sl m, k1, sl1 wyib, pl Tm, turn.

Short Row 2 (WS): P2, sl m, work in Twisted Rib to next m, sl m, k1, [p to next m, sl m] three times, work in Twisted Rib to next m, sl m, k1, p1, s1 wyif, pl Tm, turn.

Short Row 3: Knit to 1 st before m, m1-L, p1, sl m, work in Twisted Rib to next m, sl m, m1-R, knit to next m, sl m, ssk, knit to 2 sts before next m, k2tog, sl m, knit to 1 st before next m, m1-L, p1, sl m, work in Twisted Rib to next m, sl m, m1-R, knit to Tm, remove Tm, k1, sl1 wyib, pl Tm, turn—2 sts inc'd.

Short Row 4: Purl to m, sl m, work in Twisted Rib to next m, sl

m, k1, [p to next m, sl m] three times, work in Twisted Rib to next m, sl m, k1, purl to Tm, remove Tm, p1, s1 wyif, pl Tm, turn. Repeat Short Rows 3 & 4 another 2 (4, 1, 3, 5, 2, 4) times—204 (232, 250, 278, 306, 324, 356) sts.

Increase rows

Short Row 5: Knit to 1 st before m, p1, sl m, work in Twisted Rib to next m, sl m, m1-R, knit to next m, sl m, ssk, knit to 2 sts before next m, k2tog, sl m, knit to 1 st before next m, m1-L, p1, sl-m, work in Twisted Rib to next m, sl m, knit to Tm, remove Tm, k1, sl1 wyib, pl Tm, turn.

Short Row 6: Purl to m, sl m, work in Twisted Rib to next m, sl m, k1, [purl to next m, sl m] three times, work in Twisted Rib to next m, sl m, k1, purl to Tm, remove Tm, p1, s1 wyif, pl Tm, turn.

Short Row 7: Knit to 1 st before m, m1-L, p1, sl m, work in Twisted Rib to next m, sl m, m1-R, knit to next m, sl m, ssk, knit to 2 sts before next m, k2tog, sl m, k to 1 st before next m, m1-L, p1, sl-m, work in Twisted Rib to next m, sl m, m1-R, knit to Tm, remove Tm, k1, sl1 wyib, pl Tm, turn—2 sts inc'd.

Short Row 8: Purl to m, sl m, work in Twisted Rib to next m, sl m, k1, [purl to next m, sl m] three times, work in Twisted Rib to next m, sl m, k1, purl to Tm, remove Tm, p1, s1 wyif, pl Tm, turn. Repeat Short Rows 7 & 8 another 1 (1, 2, 2, 2, 3, 3) times. Work this 6 (6, 8, 8, 8, 10, 10) row sequence four more times—224 (252, 280, 308, 336, 364, 396) sts.

Join for working in the rnd (short rows are now finished, continue in the rnd from this point on).

Rnd 9 (RS): Knit to 1 st before m, p1, sl m, work in Twisted Rib to next m, sl m, m1-R, knit to next m, sl m, ssk, knit to 2 sts before next m, k2tog, sl m, knit to 1 st before next m, m1-L, p1, sl-m, work in Twisted Rib to next m, sl m, knit to Tm, remove Tm, k1.

You are now at 2nd Tm, Tm now marks the beginning of the rnd.

Rnd 10 (RS): Knit to 1 st before m, p1, sl m, work in Twisted Rib to next m, sl m, [knit to next m, sl m] three times, p1, work in Twisted Rib to next m, sl m, knit to Tm, sl Tm.

Rnd 11: Knit to 1 st before m, m1-L, p1, sl m, work in Twisted Rib to next m, sl m, m1-R, knit to next m, sl m, ssk, knit to 2 sts before next m, k2tog, sl m, knit to 1 st before next m, m1-L, p1, sl-m, work in Twisted Rib to next m, sl m, m1-R, knit to 2 sts before next m, s2kpoM.

Rnd 12: Knit to 1 st before m, p1, sl m, work in Twisted Rib to next m, sl m, [knit to next m, sl m] three times, p1, work in Twisted Rib to next m, sl m, knit to Tm, sl Tm. Repeat Rnds 11 & 12 another 1 (1, 2, 2, 2, 3, 3) times.

Rnd 13 (RS): Knit to 1 st before m, p1, sl m, work in Twisted Rib to next m sl m, m1-R, knit to next m, sl m, ssk, knit to 2 sts before next m, k2tog, sl m, knit to 1 st before next m, m1-L, p1, sl-m, work in Twisted Rib to next m, sl m, knit to 2 sts before Tm, s2kpoM—2 sts dec'd.

Rnd 14: Knit to 1 st before m, p1, sl m, work in Twisted Rib to next m, sl m, [knit to next m, sl m] three times, p1, work in Twisted Rib to next m, sl m, knit to Tm, sl Tm. Work this 6 (6, 8, 8, 8, 10, 10) rnd sequence once more—220 (248, 276, 304, 332, 360, 392) sts in total.

Rnd 15: Knit to 1 st before m, m1-L, p1, sl m, work in Twisted Rib to next m, sl m, m1-R, knit to next m, sl m, ssk, knit to 2 sts before next m, k2tog, sl m, k to 1 st before next m, m1-L, p1, sl-m, work in Twisted Rib to next m, sl m, m1-R, knit to 2 sts before Tm, s2kpoM.

Rnd 16: Knit to 1 st before m, p1, sl m, work in Twisted Rib to next m, sl m, [knit to next m, sl m] three times, p1, work in Twisted Rib to next m, sl m, knit to Tm, sl Tm.
Repeat Rnds 15 & 16 another 4 (5, 5, 6, 7, 6, 4) times.

Final rounds of lower gusset

Rnd 17: Knit to 1 st before m, m1-L, p1, sl m, work in Twisted Rib to next m, sl m, m1-R, knit to next m, remove m, s2kpo, sl m, knit to 1 st before next m, m1-L, p1, sl-m, work in Twisted Rib to next m, sl m, m1-R, knit to 2 sts before Tm, s2kpoM.

Rnd 18: Knit to 1 st before m, p1, sl m, work in Twisted Rib to next m, sl m, [knit to next m, sl m] twice, p1, work in Twisted Rib to next m, sl m, knit to Tm, sl Tm.

Remainder of Body

Rnd 19: *Knit to 1 st before m, m1-L, p1, sl m, work in Twisted Rib to next m, sl m, m1-R, knit to 2 sts before next m, s2kpoM, rep from * once more.

Rnd 20: Knit to 1 st before m, p1, sl m, work in Twisted Rib to next m, sl m, [knit to next m, sl m] twice, p1, work in Twisted Rib to next m, sl m, knit to Tm, sl Tm.
Work rnds 19 & 20 another 12 (9, 6, 4, 2, 0, 0) times.

Sleeves

Bind off armpits

Rnd 1: *Knit to 1 st before m, p1, remove m, bind off to next m, including the purled stitch from before the marker, remove m, knit to 2 sts before next m, s2kpoM, rep from * once more, knit to bind off, this is now the beginning of the rnd—194 (218, 242, 266, 290, 314, 338) sts equally divided between back and front.

Cast on for sleeves

Rnd 2: Pl m, *using backward loop method CO 24 (24, 26, 27, 28, 33, 33) sts, pl m, CO 10 (12, 14, 16, 18, 20, 24) sts, pl m, CO 23 (23, 25, 26, 27, 32, 32) sts, k1, pl m, [knit to next m, sl m] twice, rep from * once more—308 (336, 372, 404, 436, 484, 516) sts in total.

Rnd 3: *Knit to 1 st before m, p1, sl m, work in Twisted Rib to next m, sl m, [knit to 2 sts before next m, s2kpoM] three times, rep from * once more—12 sts dec'd.

Rnd 4: *Knit to 1 st before m, p1, sl m, work in Twisted Rib to next m, sl m, [knit to next m, sl m] three times, rep from * once more.
Work rnds 3 & 4 another 0 (1, 2, 3, 4, 5, 6) times.

Rnd 5: Knit to 1 st before m, p1, sl m, work in Twisted Rib to next m, sl m, knit to 2 sts before next m, s2kpoM, removing marker entirely, knit to 2 sts before next m, s2kpoM, knit to 2 sts before next m, s2kpoM, removing marker entirely, knit to 1 st before m, p1, sl m, work in Twisted Rib to next m, sl m, knit to 2 sts before next m, s2kpoM, removing marker entirely, [knit to 2 sts before next m, s2kpoM] twice—12 sts dec'd—284 (300, 324, 344, 364, 400, 420) sts in total.

Rnd 6: *Knit to 1 st before m, p1, sl m, work in Twisted Rib to next m, sl m, knit to next m, sl m, rep from * once more, knit to next m, sl m.

Rnd 7: *Knit to 1 st before m, p1, sl m, work in Twisted Rib to next m, sl m, knit to 2 sts before next m, s2kpoM, rep from * once more, knit to next m—4 sts dec'd.
Work rnds 6 & 7 another 3 (3, 5, 5, 6, 7, 7) times—268 (284, 300, 320, 336, 368, 388) sts.

Place markers in preparation for Rockefeller Center Motif

Rnd 8: Knit to 1 st before m, p1, sl m, work in Twisted Rib to next m, sl m, knit to next m, sl m, knit to 1 st before m, p1, sl m, work in Twisted Rib to next m, sl m, k25 (27, 32, 36, 34, 42, 45), pl m, knit to next m, sl m, k 37 (37, 37, 37, 43, 43, 43), pl m, knit to next m, sl m.

Rockefeller Center Motif section

In the next rnd, stitches are bound off to begin the drop stitch motif. Each bind off starts by increasing 1 st, this extra st is then bound off along with 6 other sts.

Rnd 1: Knit to 1 before m, p1, sl m, work in Twisted Rib to next m, sl m, knit to 2 sts before next m, s2kpoM, knit to 1 st before m, p1, sl m, work in Twisted Rib to next m, sl m, knit to next m, sl m, *kfb, [k1, pass 1 over] seven times, k4, rep from * 2 (2, 2, 2, 3, 3, 3) more times, s2kpoM, *k4, kfb, [k1, pass 1 over] seven times, rep from * 2 (2, 2, 2, 3, 3, 3) more times, sl m, knit to next m—40 (40, 40, 40, 52, 52, 52) sts dec'd.

In the next rnd, 2 sts are cast on above each bind off using the backwards loop CO. Before starting the neck, these sts will be dropped to create the ladders in the motif.

Rnd 2: Knit to 1 st before m, p1, sl m, work in Twisted Rib to next m, sl m, knit to next m, knit to 1 st before m, p1, sl m, work in Twisted Rib to next m, sl m, knit to next m, sl m, *k1-b, CO 2, k1-b, k4, rep from * 2 (2, 2, 2, 3, 3, 3) more times, k1, sl m, *k4, k1-b, CO 2, k1-b, rep from * 2 (2, 2, 2, 3, 3, 3) more times, sl m, knit to next m, sl m—12 (12, 12, 12, 16, 16, 16) sts inc'd—240 (256, 272, 292, 300, 332, 352) sts

Rnd 3: Knit to 1 st before m, p1, sl m, work in Twisted Rib to next m, sl m, knit to 2 sts before next m, s2kpoM, knit to 1 st before m, p1, sl m, work in Twisted Rib to next m, sl m, knit to next m, sl m, work Rockefeller Center Motif chart, sl m, knit to next m—4 sts dec'd.

Rnd 4: Knit to 1 st before m, p1, sl m, work in Twisted Rib to next m, sl m, knit to next m, knit to 1 st before m, p1, sl m, work in Twisted Rib to next m, knit to next m, sl m, work Rockefeller Center Motif chart, sl m, knit to next m, sl m. Work this two rnd sequence 3 (2, 1, 1, 1, 2, 1) more times—224 (244, 264, 284, 292, 320, 344) sts.

Rnd 5: Knit to 3 sts before m, ssk, p1, sl m, work in Twisted Rib to next m, sl m, k2tog, knit to 2 sts before next m, s2kpoM, knit to 3 sts before m, ssk, p1, sl m, work in Twisted Rib to next m, sl m, k2tog, knit to next m, sl m, work Rockefeller Center Motif chart, sl m, knit to next m, sl m—8 sts dec'd.

Rnd 6: Knit to 1 st before m, p1, sl m, work in Twisted Rib to next m, sl m, knit to next m, sl m, knit to 1 st before m, p1, sl m, work in Twisted Rib to next m, sl m, knit to next m, sl m, work Rockefeller Center Motif chart, sl m, knit to next m, sl m. Work this two rnd sequence 9 (10, 11, 11, 11, 10, 11) more times—144 (156, 168, 188, 196, 232, 248) sts in total.

Neck

Rnd 7: Knit to 3 sts before m, ssk, p1, sl m, work in Twisted Rib to next m, k2tog, knit to 2 sts before next m, s2kpoM, knit to 3 sts before m, ssk, p1, sl m, work in Twisted Rib to next m, sl m,

k2tog, knit to next m, sl m, work Rockefeller Center Motif chart, sl m, knit to next m, sl m—8 sts dec'd.

Rnd 8: Knit to 1 st before m, p1, remove m, work in Twisted Rib to next m, remove m, k14 (16, 18, 22, 19, 27, 29), BO 43 (43, 43, 43, 55, 55, 55) removing marker halfway through BO, knit to 1 st before m, p1, remove m, work in Twisted Rib to next m, remove m, knit to next m, remove m, work Rockefeller Center Motif chart, remove m, knit to next m, remove m.

I-Cord Bindoff

Slip sts along ndl to BO section. CO 3 sts onto right ndl. Work 3 rows of I-cord (see Techniques, p. 67), work I-cord BO to edge of motif section; *work 6 rows of i-cord over the ladder, then 1 row I-cord BO to pick up the next stitch; repeat from * to end of motif section 5 (5, 5, 5, 7, 7, 7) more times; work I-cord BO on remaining neck sts, work 4 ¾ (4 ¾, 4 ¾, 4 ¾, 6, 6, 6) inches/12 (12, 12, 12, 15, 15, 15) cm of i-cord, break yarn, then neatly sew ends of I-cord together.

Sleeves

Pick up and knit 68 (72, 80, 86, 92, 106, 114) sts around armhole and distribute sts equally between DPNs. Purl 1 rnd, knit 1 rnd, p1 rnd. BO loosely. Repeat on opposite armhole.

FINISHING

Weave in all ends. Hang on a plastic hanger and steam gently until sts are even in appearance and neck motif is even and flat.

Rockefeller Center Motif

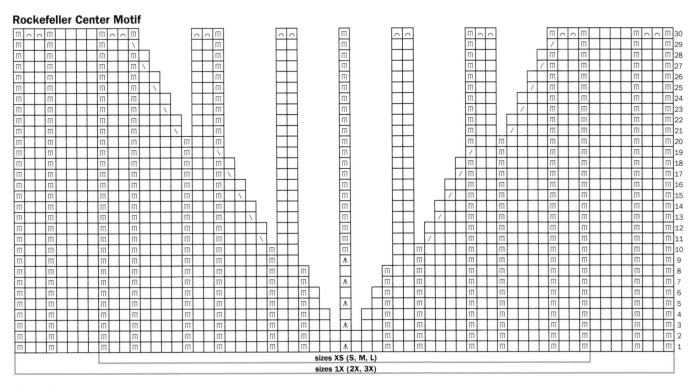

sizes XS (S, M, L)

sizes 1X (2X, 3X)

Chart Key

☐ = knit ⋀ = s2kpoM

╱ = k2tog ⅲ = k1-b

╲ = ssk ⌒ = k1 then drop st from ndl

Sheep Meadow

Lars Rains

One of my favorite ways to spend a lazy afternoon in New York City is to stroll around Central Park. I would park myself on a bench and just watch people pass by. The Sheep Meadow is a beloved section of the park for New Yorkers. On any given day, you can see people lying out on their blankets or flying their kites there. It was actually home at the turn of the last century to a flock of sheep that would trim the grass and fertilize the lawn. These sheep were housed in a Victorian building that would later become the Tavern on the Green restaurant.

For this long funnel cowl, I wanted to represent the undulating ground of the park using balanced pairs of short row sections and uneven stripes. It will definitely keep you warm as you enjoy this little piece of nature in the heart of the city.

Size
One Size

Finished Measurements
Length: 76 inches/193 cm
Width: 12 inches/30.5 cm

Materials
Backyard Fiberworks Prairie Take Five Gradient Kit (100% superwash merino; 200 yd/183 m per 1.75 oz/50 g skein);
   color: Lichen; 1 kit
     Color A: Dark Green; 1 skein
     Color B: Medium Green; 1 skein
     Color C: Light Green; 1 skein
     Color D: Medium Yellow; 1 skein
     Color E: Light Yellow; 1 skein
US4/3.5mm 60-inch/150-cm circular needle (or one size smaller than gauge needle)
US5/3.75mm 60-inch/150-cm circular needle (or size needed to achieve gauge)
4 stitch markers, with 1 unique marker to indicate beginning of round, tapestry needle

Gauge
21 sts x 37 rounds = 4 inches/10 cm in Stockinette Stitch with larger needle, after blocking

PATTERN

First Ribbing Section

With smaller ndl and Color A, CO 400 sts. Join together in the rnd, being careful not to twist. Place m to indicate BOR.

Rnd 1: (K2, p2) around.

Repeat Rnd 1 nine more times.

Switch to larger ndl and knit 1 rnd.

Set-Up Rnd: K100, pl m, k100, pl m, k100, pl m, k100.

First Short Row Section

Short Row 1 (RS): Knit to 90 sts past second m, turn.

Note: Each of Short Rows 2–18 increase the stitch count by one—17 sts inc'd.

Short Row 2 (WS): Bytb, purl to 90 sts past m, turn.

Short Row 3: Bytf, knit to 80 sts past m, turn.

Short Row 4: Bytb, purl to 80 sts past m, turn.

Short Row 5: Bytf, knit to 70 sts past m, turn.

Short Row 6: Bytb, purl to 70 sts past m, turn.

Short Row 7: Bytf, knit to 60 sts past m, turn.

Short Row 8: Bytb, purl to 60 sts past m, turn.

Short Row 9: Bytf, knit to 50 sts past m, turn.

Short Row 10: Bytb, purl to 50 sts past m, turn.

Short Row 11: Bytf, knit to 40 sts past m, turn.

Short Row 12: Bytb, purl to 40 sts past m, turn.

Short Row 13: Bytf, knit to 30 sts past m, turn.

Short Row 14: Bytb, purl to 30 sts past m, turn.

Short Row 15: Bytf, knit to 20 sts past m, turn.

Short Row 16: Bytb, purl to 20 sts past m, turn.

Short Row 17: Bytf, knit to 10 sts past m, turn.

Short Row 18: Bytb, purl to 10 sts past m, turn.

Short Row 19: Bytf, knit to m, (k9, k2tog) nine times, knit to 90 sts past BOR m, turn—9 sts dec'd and 1 st inc'd.

Short Rows 20–36: Repeat Short Rows 2–18—17 sts inc'd.

Short Row 37 (RS): Bytf, knit to BOR m—1 st inc'd.

Resume working in the rnd.

Rnd 1: (K9, k2tog) nine times, knit to 9 sts past first m, (ssk, k10) nine times, knit to 9 sts past third m, (ssk, k10) nine times, knit to BOR m—27 sts dec'd.

Rnd 2: Knit 1 rnd.

Break Color A.

Striped Section

Carry yarns not in use loosely up inside of cowl.

Join in Color B and knit 12 rnds.

Join in Color D and knit 4 rnds.

Switch to Color B and knit 4 rnds.

Switch to Color D and knit 4 rnds.

Switch to Color B and knit 4 rnds.

Switch to Color D and knit 4 rnds.

Switch to Color B and knit 4 rnds. Break Color B.

Switch to Color D and knit 2 rnds.

Join in Color C and knit 2 rnds.

Switch to Color D and knit 2 rnds.

Switch to Color C and knit 2 rnds.

Switch to Color D and knit 2 rnds.

Switch to Color C and knit 4 rnds.

Switch to Color D and knit 4 rnds.

Switch to Color C and knit 4 rnds.

Switch to Color D and knit 2 rnds. Break Color D.

Switch to Color C and knit 12 rnds. Break Color C.

Second Short Row Section

Join in Color E and work section as follows:

Knit 2 rnds.

Short Row 1 (RS): Knit to 10 sts past first m, turn.

Short Row 2 (WS): Bytb, purl to 10 sts past m, turn—1 st inc'd.

Note: Each of Short Rows 3–19 increase and decrease the stitch count by one.

Short Row 3: Bytf, knit to 9 sts past m, k2tog, k10, turn.

Short Row 4: Bytb, purl to 9 sts past m, ssp, p10, turn.

Short Row 5: Bytf, knit to 19 sts past m, k2tog, k10, turn.

Short Row 6: Bytb, purl to 19 sts past m, ssp, p10, turn.

Short Row 7: Bytf, knit to 29 sts past m, k2tog, k10, turn.

Short Row 8: Bytb, purl to 29 sts past m, ssp, p10, turn.

Short Row 9: Bytf, knit to 39 sts past m, k2tog, k10, turn.

Short Row 10: Bytb, purl to 39 sts past m, ssp, p10, turn.

Short Row 11: Bytf, knit to 49 sts past m, k2tog, k10, turn.

Short Row 12: Bytb, purl to 49 sts past m, ssp, p10, turn.

Short Row 13: Bytf, knit to 59 sts past m, k2tog, k10, turn.

Short Row 14: Bytb, purl to 59 sts past m, ssp, p10, turn.

Short Row 15: Bytf, knit to 69 sts past m, k2tog, k10, turn.

Short Row 16: Bytb, purl to 69 sts past m, ssp, p10, turn.

Short Row 17: Bytf, knit to 79 sts past m, k2tog, k10, turn.

Short Row 18: Bytb, purl to 79 sts past m, ssp, p10, turn.

Short Row 19: Bytf, knit to 89 sts past m, k2tog, k10 sts past third m, turn.

Short Rows 20–36: Repeat Short Rows 2–18—16 sts dec'd and 17 sts inc'd.

Short Row 37 (RS): Bytf, knit to 89 sts past m, k2tog, knit to BOR m—1 st dec'd and 1 st inc'd.

Resume working in the rnd.

Rnd 1: K9, ssk, knit to 9 sts after second m, ssk, knit to BOR m—2 sts dec'd.

Rnd 2: Knit 1 rnd.

Second Ribbing Section

Switch to smaller ndl and work section as follows:

Rnd 1: (K2, p2) around.

Repeat Rnd 1 nine more times.

BO loosely in pattern.

FINISHING

Weave in all ends with tapestry needle. Block to finished measurements.

Knit Yorkers

Brittney Bailey

Email: *bwoolensknits@gmail.com*
Instagram: *@b.woolens*
Ravelry: *bwoolens*

Brittney Bailey is a knitwear designer and fiber enthusiast who hails from the Pacific Northwest. She has been knitting for over fifteen years and has had the good fortune to work and teach in incredible yarn shops like Dublin Bay Knitting Co (Portland, Oregon) and Purl Soho (New York!). Her knitwear designs are heavily inspired by the needs of her daily life. She is constantly in pursuit of "that perfect sweater"—that will work for every occasion. She is currently based in New York City where she spent the last year managing Purl Soho's brick-and-mortar location. She is currently working on a Ph.D. in Art History with special interests in feminism and portraiture, while she continues to publish her own designs and serve as social media coordinator for Purl Soho. Her favorite thing about living in New York City is being able to visit the Met whenever she wants.

Lisa Chamoff

Email: *lisa@indieuntangled.com*
Instagram: *@indieuntangled*
Ravelry: *LisaKC*

Lisa has lived in New York City since 2002, first in Manhattan and now in Ditmas Park, Brooklyn. In 2014, after more than a decade as a newspaper reporter, Lisa launched Indie Untangled (*indieuntangled.com*), a marketplace and blog that promotes the work of yarn dyers, pattern designers, and crafters of knitting-related accessories. She also organizes the annual Rhinebeck Trunk Show, held the weekend of the New York State Sheep & Wool Festival. When she's not running the site, or knitting shawls and sweaters, Lisa works as a freelance writer specializing in home design, real estate, and healthcare.

Kathleen Dames

Email: *kathleen@kathleendames.com*
Instagram: *@kathleendames*
Ravelry: *Purly*

Kathleen Dames focuses on flattering designs and knitterly details for the garments and accessories she creates for her own pattern line, as well as publications such as *Knitty*, *Jane Austen Knits*, and *Interweave Knits*. From her first large-scale knitting project (a poncho from Melanie Falick's *Weekend Knitting*), she has been making patterns her own, thanks to her personal style and the wisdom of Elizabeth Zimmermann. Kathleen is cocreator of *Filament*, a quarterly knitting pattern collection filled of modern classics and a vintage sensibility, with Anne Podlesak of Wooly Wonka Fibers. She hosts the podcast *The Sweater with Kathleen Dames* on YouTube, where you will learn to knit a sweater in twelve weeks. Kathleen worked as an art director in book publishing for many years prior to embarking on a career in knitwear design. Having celebrated #tenyearsanewyorker in late 2017, she has lived there long enough to be a New Yorker but is still excited by all the wonders the city holds. Find more of her work at *kathleendames.com*.

Kay Gardiner

Email: *kay@masondixonknitting.com*
Instagram: *@kaygardiner*
Ravelry: *KayGardiner*

Fifty-something New Yorker. Kay blogs daily with pal Ann Shayne at *masondixonknitting.com*, and also writes (with this same wonderful Ann Shayne) a series of small, delicious books, the *Mason-Dixon Knitting Field Guides*. Kay is always prowling for ideas on translating quilts into knitting. She loves Rowan Denim Yarn, knitting it and destroying it with bleach, sandpaper, etc. She knits a lot and is a devotee of the Alabama Chanin style of handstitched clothing. She has been known to hook a rug in the primitive (very primitive) style, usually just after getting home from Rhinebeck.

Kirsten Kapur

Email: *throughtheloops@gmail.com*
Instagram: *@throughtheloops*
Ravelry: *throughtheloops*

Kirsten Kapur is a New York City-based designer who grew up in a family of knitters, sewers, and crafters. It was only natural that she pursue a career as an apparel and textile designer in the ready-to-wear industry, where she honed her skills in garment construction and surface design. Years later, this knowledge proved invaluable when she began to experiment with the interplay between fiber colors and textures in her original knitwear designs and patterns. Visit her website at *kirstenkapurdesigns.com*.

Alice O'Reilly

Email: *alice@backyardfiberworks*
Instagram: *@backyardfiberworks*
Ravelry: *AliceOKnitty*

Alice has always been a maker. A serious dyed in the wool, hot glue burns on her fingertips, glitter in her eyebrows maker. So when she first thought about dyeing yarn, it was in the context of making stuff to support her knitting habit. She fired up her first dye pot and wow, was it not what she expected. True to form, she did no research. It was way too light and way too dark and way too not what was expected. But, also true to form, she kept trying. Alice threw a few more skeins in the pot. She read a few (okay a lot, she works at a library) of books about dyeing and yarn and how the two work together. Alice joined Ravelry groups and marveled at everyone else's perfect skeins. She started stalking hand-dyers on Instagram and Etsy. And then slowly she started getting more predictable results. More repeatable colorways. And it turns out she loved playing with color as much as she loved playing with yarn. And that's how Backyard Fiberworks began. Check out more of her yarn at *backyardfiberworks.com*

Xandy Peters

Email: *XandyPeters@gmail.com*
Instagram: *@xandypeters*
Ravelry: *saxarocks*

Xandy Peters is a knitting designer and teacher, best known as the innovator of the stacked stitch technique and for her Fox Paws pattern. Starting out as a footwear and product designer, Xandy turned to knitting as a way to explore textiles and surfaces without using factory production. She has since made a career out of knitting, publishing new patterns monthly, and teaching workshops across the country. Find Xandy online at *xandypeters.com*.

Lars Rains

Email: *modernlopi@gmail.com*
Instagram: *@modernlopi*
Ravelry: *ModernLopi*

Even though Lars Rains has been knitting for over twenty years, he still learns something new with each project he completes. He firmly believes that every knitter has the potential to become a fabulous designer with the proper tools and techniques. His design work has been featured in *Vogue Knitting*, *Rib Magazine*, *Knit Edge*, *PLY Magazine*, and *Knitty*. Lars published his first book of Icelandic patterns in 2015 and his second book of bulky accessories in 2016. He can be found online at *modernlopi.com*.

Gale Zucker

Email: *gale@gzucker.com*
Instagram: *@galezucker*
Ravelry: *SheShootsSheep*

Gale Zucker is an award-winning commercial & editorial photographer. She also happens to be a lifelong knitter and maker. Gale mashes these passions to create lifestyle fashion photography in the knitwear and handmade world. Gale brings her love of the storytelling style of photography, honed as a contributor to *The New York Times* and national magazines, to shoot narrative imagery of garments and designs. Her clients include yarn companies, book publishers, designers, magazines, and ready-to-wear clothing manufacturers and shops. Gale is the co-author/photographer of the books *Drop Dead Easy Knits*, *Craft Activism*, and *Shear Spirit*. She also teaches workshops on photography for social media, and marketing, for indie businesses and makers. Gale can found be online at *gzucker.com* and at She Shoots Sheep Shots (*ezisus.blogspot.com*), her long running blog. In real life, she can be found with her family in coastal Connecticut.

Thanks!

Penelope Dames (photography assistant's assistant), Corrina Ferguson (technical editor), Isobel Fivel (stunt coordinator), Rebecca Fox (model), Kristy Glass (documentarian), Laurel Johnson (illustrator), Kristen Lasky (location support), Liz Rolle (technical illustrator), Ann Shayne (moral support), Yliana Tibitoski (photography assistant), our family & friends for all their love and support, and

The City of New York + Knit Yorkers Everywhere

DESIGNS YOU LOVE TO KNIT
KNITS YOU LOVE TO WEAR

kathleen dames
knitwear design

kathleendames.com

Hudson Heights
The Cloisters
Fort Tryon Park

Harlem
Double Dutch Espresso
Lenox Avenue
The Studio Museum in Harlem

Upper West Side
Knitty City
The Mermaid Inn
Metropolitan Opera

Garment District
Bonchon Chicken
Mood Designer
   Fabrics
M&J Trimming
Pacific Trimming &
   Riri Zipper
Sil Thread Inc.

Central Park
Sheep Meadow

Upper East Side
Annie & Company
Go Lightly
Metropolitan Museum of Art
String Yarns
Tender Buttons

Midtown
42nd & Lex
Chrysler Building
Empire State Building
Grand Central Terminal
Grom
Kinokuniya
Madison Square Park
Manhattanhenge
Molyvos
New York Public Library
NYC Ferry
Old Town Bar
Opal Clock
The Oyster Bar at
   Grand Central
Rockefeller Center
Riverpark
Souvlaki GR Midtown
Tia Pol
Waterfront Ale House

Greenwich Village
Freud NYC
Grom
Jane Jacobs
John's Pizzeria on Bleecker Street
Merchant's House Museum
Mermaid Oyster Bar
Textile Arts Center
Washington Square Park

East Village
Downtown Yarns
Ippudo NY
The Mermaid Inn
Momofuku Noodle Bar
Souvlaki GR
The Strand
Veselka

Soho
Mariebelle
Purl Soho

Tribeca
Terroir Tribeca

Lower East Side
Katz's Delicatessen
Souvlaki GR
The Tenement Museum

Financial District
Bennie Thai Cafe

World Trade Center
Grom
NYC Ferry

New York Harbor
Ellis Island
Governors Island
Island Oyster
Statue of Liberty

Brooklyn

Argyle Yarn Shop
Bar Chord
Brooklyn Botanic Garden
Brooklyn General Store
Brooklyn Museum
Brooklyn Public Library

Brooklyn Shoe Space
Colonie
Dekalb Market Hall
Frankie's Spuntino
Freek's Mill
Hinterlands Bar

NYC Ferry
Prospect Park
Quathra Cafe
String Thing Studio
Van Brunt Stillhouse
Woolyn

Abbreviations

-b = into the back of the stitch

BO = bindoff

BOR = beginning of round

bytb = bring yarn to back

bytf = bring yarn to front

cn = cable needle

CO = caston

dec('d) = decrease(d)

DPN = double-pointed needle

inc('d) = increase(d)

k = knit

kfb = knit into the front and back of one stitch—1 stitch increased

kfbf = knit into the front, then back, then front of the same stitch—2 stitches increased

k2tog = knit two stitches together—1 stitch decreased

k2tog-b = knit two stitches together through the back loops—1 stitch decreased

k3tog = knit three stitches together—2 stitches decreased

k-wise = knitwise

m = marker

m1-L = make one stitch using backwards loop—1 stitch increased

m1-R = make one stitch using backwards loop twisted in the opposite direction of m1-L—1 stitch increased

p = purl

pl = place

p-wise = purlwise

p2tog = purl two stitches together—1 stitch decreased

rnd(s) = round(s)

RS = right side or public side of work

skp = slip one stitch knitwise, knit one stitch, pass slipped stitch over—1 stitch decreased

sk2p = slip one stitch knitwise, knit two stitches together, pass slipped stitch over—2 stitches decreased

sl = slip

ssk = slip first stitch knitwise, slip second stitch knitwise, knit two stitches together—1 stitch decreased

st(s) = stitch(es)

s2kpo = slip two stitches knitwise, knit one stitch, pass slipped stitches over—2 stitches decreased

s2kpoM (while moving marker) = beginning two stitches before next marker, slip two stitches together knitwise, remove marker, knit one stitch, pass two slipped stitches over, place marker—2 stitches decreased

Tm = Travelling marker

wyif = with yarn in front of work

wyib = with yarn in back of work

WS = wrong side or back of work

w+t = wrap and turn

yo = yarn over—1 stitch increased

Stitches

Garter Stitch (worked flat)
Knit all sts, all rows.

Stockinette Stitch (worked flat)
Row 1 (RS): Knit all sts.
Row 2 (WS): Purl all sts.

Stockinette Stitch (worked in the round)
Knit all sts, all rounds.

Twisted Rib Pattern
Row 1 (RS): *K1-b, p1, rep from *.
Row 2 (WS): *K1, p1-b, rep from *.

Techniques

Cabled Caston: *Insert right needle into space between first and second stitches on the left needle, knit one stitch onto the right needle, then place stitch onto the left needle; repeat from * as specified in pattern.

Double I-Cord Bindoff: *K1-b, k1 from right i-cord edge, k3tog-b (last st of i-cord with first two body sts to be bound off). Slip 3 sts back to left ndl and repeat from *.

I-cord: CO 3 sts. *Slip 3 sts to left ndl (or slide to other end of DPN) without twisting, k3; repeat from * as specified in pattern.

I-cord Bindoff (Single): Using Cabled Caston technique, CO 3 sts onto left needle. *K2, k2tog-b, sl3 p-wise wyib to left needles; repeat from * until all sts have been bound off.

Kitchener Stitch
- Stockinette-based sts: Bring tapestry needle through front st as if to purl, back st as if to knit, *front st as if to knit then remove stitch from knitting ndl, next front st as if to purl, back st as if to purl then remove st from knitting ndl, next back st as if to knit; repeat from * to end.
- Reverse Stockinette-based sts: Bring tapestry needle through front st as if to knit, back st as if to purl, *front st as if to purl then remove st from knitting ndl, next front st as if to knit, back st as if to knit then remove st from knitting ndl, next front st as if to purl; repeat from * to end.
- Garter-based sts: Bring tapestry needle through front st as if to purl, back st as if to purl, *front st as if to knit then remove st from knitting ndl, next front st as if to purl, back st as if to knit then remove st from knitting ndl, next front st as if to purl; repeat from * to end.

Side I-Cord
Rows 1 & 2: K1-b, k2; work in patt to last 3 sts; wyif slip last 3 sts p-wise.
Rows 3 & 4: K1-b, k2, slip 3 just-worked sts back to left ndl, k1-b, k2; work in patt to last 3 sts; wyif slip last 3 sts p-wise.

Pattern Index

CPSIA information can be obtained
at www.ICGtesting.com
Printed in the USA
BVHW06n1055270918
528486BV00003B/26/P